WEDDINGS

THE "HOW TO" MANUAL

for

NON-DENOMINATIONAL MINISTERS

and

CHAPLAINS

AND WHAT SHOULD BE DISCUSSED
WITH COUPLES
PLANNING THEIR WEDDING

John E. Fforbes-Cunningham

Library of Congress Catalog Card Number 93-90542   SAN 297-9519

ISBN 0-9637049-1-5

Published by: Anglican Publications
                   P.O. Box 208
                   Bellflower
                   California 90707-0208

Printed and bound in the
United States of America

JOHN E. FFORBES-CUNNINGHAM

WEDDINGS: THE "HOW TO" MANUAL

for Non-Denominational Ministers and Chaplains

Anglican Publications
Bellflower, California, U.S.A.

WARNING - DISCLAIMER

-o0o-

CONTENTS

CONTENTS

Page

CONTENTS

CONTENTS

Page

-o0o-

First and foremost, this "How To" book is *not intended* for the guidance of any *Priest, Minister, or Pastor* of any of the major Christian denominations [e.g. Roman Catholic, Anglican (Church of England, Episcopalian), Lutheran, Presbyterian, Baptist, Methodist, etc.,] all of whom should be experienced, and know perfectly well how to officiate in the

"Solemnization of Holy Matrimony."

In the United States of America, with the "separation of Church and State", the Law has allowed all manner of 'Religions' and 'Churches' to be established [some with names that defy interpretation] and, almost anyone to become an 'Ordained Minister' and legally entitled to prefix his (or her) name with the title of *"Reverend"*.

In many cases, individuals have become a 'Reverend' and/or even established their own 'Church' - technically anyway - for no better reason than for purposes of avoiding or minimizing personal taxation.   This book is also therefore *not intended* for the likes of them !

On the other hand, there are many legally 'Ordained Ministers' of Religion who are unable to afford the time to undertake the long study in Divinity and training required by the 'established' churches in order to become a Priest, Minister, or Pastor.   There are also those who find themselves disatisfied with the 'established' churches, or their forms and content of training for ordination and ministry.   In such situations they become ordained as a *"Non-denominational Minister."*

Such non-denominational Ministers are equally sincere in their beliefs and desire to serve their congregations and God.   In many cases, they can serve Our Lord well if only by specializing in officiating at Weddings – and *it is for them, that this "How To" book is primarily intended.*

> *Incidentally, all priests and pastors are in fact ministers, but not all ministers may be referred to as 'priests' - much depends on one's viewpoint.   Moreover, the expressions 'Priest' and 'Father' are not exclusive to the Holy Roman Church [or "Church of Rome"] as many Roman Catholics seem to have been led to believe.*

> *In the Church of England [Episcopal], one is also ordained a Priest, and, a priest in what is sometimes referred to as 'High Church', is correctly addressed as 'Father'.   Otherwise by his title of office, such as Vicar or Rector.   One ordained a Deacon is not yet a Priest – being one stage prior to final ordination.*

There are also some *ministers of non-liturgical churches* who have a need for guidance and suggestions vis-a-vis the Solemnization of Holy Matrimony, and for whom this book may also be helpful in meeting that need.

Sadly, there are too many "Ministers" simply making a living 'performing marriages' all over the place - who do no more than (i) accept a booking; (ii) arrive on the day at the appointed place, maybe a few minutes ahead of time to tell the couple what they're about to do;   (iii) churn out some sort of 'contemporary service' of their own, that makes the couple 'legally married';   (iv) complete the necessary certification;   (v) take the money, and (vi) depart.

Their 'Order of Service' being such that invariably, no-one will complain about its content afterwards, there being nothing in it to complain about ! These "ministers" are, in my view, simply "in it for the money" and by no stretch of the imagination, doing their duty as members of the clergy.

These same "Ministers" (and some others of certain non-liturgical churches also) cannot be bothered to meet with and discuss alternative services with a couple beforehand - certainly not to explain the meaning of all that is contained in such as the old 'Traditional' Order of Service.

In many countries, you mostly find that Catholic marries Catholic, Protestant marries Protestant and Jew marries Jew, etc.   But in the United States, you find people of almost every different faith and denomination getting married to one another - especially in the State of California !

This invariably calls for the Marriage Ceremony to take place, not in a Church, Chapel, Temple or Synagogue, but "on neutral ground".   More often than not, this is where the suitably motivated, experienced *Non-denominational Minister* comes into the picture.

The marriage can be performed almost anywhere;   if not in a Church or Chapel - then in one's own home or garden;   in an hotel or restaurant;   in a park or on the beach;   aboard a ship, yacht, or boat.

What better and bigger 'Church' can you have than out in the open under God's good sky ?   As the Bible states: "Wherever two or more are gathered together in my Name..." - there is your Church !

Coincidentally, this book may *also serve to assist couples planning on marriage,* to choose the 'Order of Service' for their Wedding - and even more importantly, to *understand what it is that they are about to pledge to each other.*   That is to say, if they want a Religious Service - to make their vows *"before God and this congregation (or company)"* - and not merely a Civil Ceremony.

The latter can of course be performed *very* quickly and simply if wishing to be married *only* "in the eyes of the State".

Marriage Services

Since this book is written primarily for *Non-Denominational Ministers,* whilst it includes a number of different Orders of Service (for marriages), selected for their consideration and use, it does not attempt to include those used by all of the many different faiths and denominations to be found in the United States of America.

> *Whilst providing the complete 'Order of Service' in a variety of forms from 'Traditional' to 'Modern' versions used in the Christian Church; along with 'Contemporary' and 'Inter-Faith' [Non-Denominational], as well as 'Secular' [Civil Law], in a 'Ready for Use' printing - the reader will observe that none of the examples given in this book cater*

to the 'trendy' or 'trivial' inclined.   All in fact, stem essentially from the 'original' marriage service - used for more than one thousand years in Christian Churches.   To quote the vernacular: "If it works, don't 'fix it'."

Where a minister is himself of any particular denomination by upbringing he might well be inclined to use the service with which he is already familiar through that upbringing - the 'Order of Service' for which he can obtain in publications produced by that particular church or society.

However, subject only to a marriage service meeting the requirements of the law obtaining in the State in which the marriage is to take place, the minister officiating can in fact use whatever Order of Service he (and the couple also) may wish to use.   He can even compose his own !

The selection contained in this book should, however, provide the minister with a sufficiently wide choice to suit almost all of the different couples for whom he - *as a non-denominational minister* - may be asked to officiate in their marriage.   Certainly from which to extract, adapt, or build upon to suit, in each case.   The opportunities for innovation, and to make a service uniquely 'personal' for any particular couple, are limitless.

Weddings in Costume ?

Whilst, as already stated, *none* of the marriage services I have included in this book cater for the 'trendy' or 'trivial' inclined - this is not to say that I am opposed to anyone having a 'special theme' for their Wedding.

I am indeed personally opposed to trendy or trivial **wording** in any marriage ceremony.   However, where the Wedding and Reception is to be **other than in a church;** providing that the couple - and all others attending - take the matter of the marriage itself seriously, and behave throughout as they would in a church, I see no reason to object to their being 'in costume' for the occasion.

By 'costume', I don't mean such as swimwear, beachwear, clowns or halloween and the like !   And equally, I am frankly opposed to marriages taking place in a frivolous atmosphere, or 'exhibitionist' manner - such as diving off a high board into a swimming pool, or parachuting out of a basket from under an hot-air baloon !

I have officiated at many weddings where the participants and most of the guests have appeared in 'costume' - dressed as Elizabethans, as Pilgrims, as Confederate Officers with their Southern Ladies, and even as Pirates - the latter, I may add, aboard an old square-rigged 'Pirate Ship' complete with cannons later being fired in 'salute' to the Bride and 'Groom !   Thus far however, I have not officiated wearing any such 'costumes' myself.

Providing only that their costumes are reasonably authentic **and in good taste** - and we bear in mind that, for the period of the marriage service itself, wherever we are, that place becomes (albeit temporarily) our 'church', in which all should **conduct themselves with decorum and due reverence of the proceedings** - I can find no fault in allowing such dress. Afterwards, then by all means, have a party and celebrate accordingly.

MARRIAGE LAWS

This chapter is (as indeed also is most of this book) specifically addressed to the Non-denominational Ministers intent upon performing marriages - *in the United States of America.*

Performing marriages is both enjoyable and satisfying.   You need have no hesitation as long as you comply with the laws and procedures applicable in your State.   It is imperative that, before you solemnize a marriage, you acquaint yourself with the laws of the State in which the marriage is to be performed.   It is usually the Office of the County Clerk that will be able to furnish you with all the information needed.

Most States do not require any particular kind of ceremony; they leave that to the church in question.   Those States that have requirements regarding the ceremony simply state that the bride and bridegroom must say to each other, in the presence of the minister and the witnesses, that they **take each other as husband and wife.**   The rest of the ceremony may be in a traditional form or may be made up by the couple and/or the minister.

> *Concerning ceremonies 'made up' by the couple.   You will undoubtedly, from time to time, be approached by a couple presenting you with their own 'script' of what they want to say and what they want you to say. Provided this includes the aforementioned requirement that they 'take each other as husband and wife', it will make their marriage legal. However, if called upon to serve them as a Minister of Religion - and not merely as someone authorized to perform marriages - you may well consider their 'script' as being (in your opinion) unacceptable as a suitable 'Religious Ceremony'.   There is nothing in Law that requires you to perform the marriage as that couple prescribes and accordingly, in your own discretion, you can refuse to do so.*
>
> *I have had couples present me with their own 'script' endeavouring to insist [!] that I use it, word-for-word as they presume to prescribe - and I have refused them.   In some cases I have felt obliged to tell them "If you can find a minister prepared to read your 'script' in its present form, then I would not consider him (or her) to be a true minister of our Lord's church !   I recommend that, if all you really want is to 'be married' - you find someone who is duly licenced to give you a Secular Ceremony [i.e. Civil Wedding] instead. "*

In some States it is required that the minister be registered and have a State Licence, the number of which must be recorded on every Marriage Certificate. In most States a licence must be issued [obtained by] each couple before marriage.   The laws vary between different States.   If a minister performs a marriage ceremony without legal warrant to do so, the marriage is valid, but the minister will be subject to fine and even imprisonment.

Before you perform a marriage ceremony, you must be certain that the couple has a valid **Marriage Licence.**   Check the licence thoroughly and, any other documents that come with it, to see what is required of you.   Usually all you have to do is to complete the blank spaces on the marriage licence itself.   There should be a space for the couple, the minister, and the witnesses to sign.   Also, you may be required to provide the couple with a **Marriage Certificate.**   When marriage certificates are required, they are often provided (by the County Clerk/Recorder/Registrar) along with the marriage licence.   You will probably be required to return the licence and other papers (if any) to the County Clerk or other official, within a certain number of days.

Never, under any circumstances whatsoever, perform a marriage ceremony unless and until you first have the couple's marriage licence safely in your personal possession.   There will be occasions when they have "forgotten to bring it" with them - everything stops right there.   Have them send someone home (or wherever) to get it.   It will not suffice that you accept an assurance that "it's on the way" - it might **not** get to you !

I had a case some years ago where the Bride had the Marriage Licence but had forgotten to bring it with her.   The Wedding was being held in her parents' home and relations of both the bridegroom's family and hers, had travelled to California from all over the Country to attend the event.   The bride had been living in lodgings in another town not too far away, so sent one of her friends 'home' to fetch the licence. The friend searched the bride's room there, all to no avail.

Meanwhile, as first one, then another hour passed, with frequent quite fruitless 'phone calls between the two.   Everyone at the 'Wedding' was becoming extremely agitated, and the bride was by then in a state of hysteria.   She had her father trying to persuade me to perform a 'Mock Wedding', and there were others of both families pressing me to proceed with the marriage anyway, on the assumption that the Marriage Licence was bound to 'turn up' sooner or later !

Eventually, I was able to get the bride to 'calm down' sufficiently to recall where and at what time she has last laid eyes on the document. "I had it on the coffee table in the common room last night at the hostel" she replied.   I then asked her "what else was on that coffee table ?"   "Oh, a lot of magazines and so forth."   At this, I 'phoned her friend who was still at the home, and asked her to check that coffee table -   "What's on it now ?"   "Nothing !"   "Check the trash bins outside."   There, crumpled up (but still readable) among the trash, she found the licence !   Fortunately, being a Saturday, the garbage trucks had not yet been around to empty the trash bins - but what if they had ?

Had I been persuaded to perform the marriage without the licence, on that Saturday, and it had not been found - they couldn't have obtained another licence until the following Monday and (although they might well have been legally married) I would have been subject to arrest, a fine or imprisonment, or both !   Don't take any such chances.

It is generally accepted that, Society has the right to know that a couple are to be recognized as living together as man and wife [some prefer the expression "husband and wife"] hence the public records maintained by the appropriate authorities.

The thoughtful minister will keep a record of all marriages at which he has officiated.   And you will be surprised how often this will in any case prove useful - especially if you note in each case which 'Order of Service' was used – when you subsequently receive referrals from couples' friends and relatives asking you to perform 'the same ceremony' for them.

The 'Confidential' Licence
[California]

The State of California has a special law which allows an unmarried man and woman who have been "living together as man and wife" to marry without a regular **"License and Certificate of Marriage"** or blood test.   If you are prepared to perform this type of marriage, you should tell the couple to go to the County Clerk's office and obtain a form called **"Authorization and Certificate of Confidential Marriage"**.   Only persons who are at least 18 years of age may be married in this manner.   The names of the couple married in this way are not published in the "Vital Statistics" section of the newspaper and, copies (of the form) are only available to the couple being married.   Anyone else must have a court order to see the form or obtain a copy, although of course, the couple may themselves provide copies to whomsoever they may wish.

The idea behind this was to provide a way for people who have been living together, to be married without the embarrassment of admitting in public that they were not really married in the first place.   This law was made in the 1800s !

> *In practice however, the majority of couples who choose to obtain a 'Confidential Licence' instead of a regular Marriage Licence, do so in order to avoid the inconvenience of time off from work (and maybe expense also) to get their blood tests done.   In any case, if they have been living together "as man and wife" for some time [six months or more], it's a trifle too late for blood tests anyway, isn't it ?*

> *If you are a Non-Denominational Minister, performing marriages more often than not "on neutral ground" rather than in a church or chapel; you'll probably find that (depending of course on the composition of the community in which you are located) a large number of your weddings will be for couples who have already been living together for some time and, who will present you with their 'Confidential Licence'. And, they will often be couples who are not too concerned whether anyone attending their Wedding happens to know that they have already been living together, or not.   Nevertheless, you should check this point with the couple beforehand so that you don't 'let the cat out of the bag' by allowing anyone to see their 'Confidential Licence' – it may even be that Mum and Dad didn't know !*

Whereas a regular Marriage Licence can be obtained anywhere in the State of California where such licences are issued, and is valid for 90 days for use anywhere within the State, and DOES have to be signed after the ceremony by (essentially one but usually two) witnesses as well as the officiating minister – on the other hand, **a 'Confidential Licence' must be obtained within the same County in which the couple are to be married, and DOES NOT have space for signatures of any witnesses at all.**   The couple are required to sign the form at time and place of issue, and you as the officiating minister must sign it after having performed the marriage ceremony.

Certified Copies

The couple will need to obtain 'Certified Copies' of their Marriage Licence [whether regular or confidential] from the County Recorder/Registrar, to show such as the Department of Motor Vehicles, Social Security and Passport Office, who will not accept photo-copies or ordinary Marriage Certificates.

Advertising

In most States you are allowed to advertise that you will perform marriages and, you may usually charge any fee you feel is appropriate. However, some States such as **Kentucky** forbid ministers to solicit marriages.

Ordained or "Licenced" Ministers

The laws of all States allow ministers to perform marriages.   In **APPENDIX ONE** you will find a summary of State Marriage Laws to advise you as to what you must do to perform marriages in your State.   Under each State you will find paraphrased what the Law has to say about ministers who may perform marriages.

Many of the States say that "ordained or licenced ministers" may perform marriages, and in this context "licenced" means licenced by the church [i.e. the church by which you were ordained as a minister.]   In addition to being ordained and licenced by (your) church, some States require the minister to be registered with the State or City before performing marriages.   If such a State or City requirement exists in your State, this is mentioned in the summary.   If there is no mention of registration, in all probability none is required by your State.   In the summary of State Laws, if you are required to keep certain records concerning marriages performed by you, this is also set down – and the official to contact if you have any other questions about performing marriages.

*The summary contained in **APPENDIX ONE** has been compiled with every effort made to be sure that it is accurate – but accuracy cannot be guaranteed.   Something may have been overlooked and, in any case, laws change from time to time and, there could be changes of which the author was not aware at this time of writing in 1991.   Therefore, you should **verify this information with your County Clerk.***

"Mail Order" Ministers

From time to time, a few places have made it difficult or impossible for "mail order" ministers to perform marriages.   The prevailing consensus however is that this is an unconstitutional practice and, since a United States Circuit Court Judge has ruled in favour of "mail order" ministers, it should be clear to all that [if this category applies to you] you are in fact legally entitled to perform marriages.

*The case in question was brought against the United States of America, Defendant [in this instance, the Internal Revenue Service] and decided in favour of the Plaintiff [the Church].   Since this was a 'Federal Case' with a United States Circuit Court Judge presiding, his ruling made the decision **applicable throughout the United States**, rather than merely applicable only in the State in which the case was heard.*

Under the Constitution of the United States, with the "separation of Church and State" who is to say that certain churches are 'legitimate' - but that the Church by which you were 'ordained' is not ?   Whatever anyone's own personal objections may be to allowing 'mail order' ministers to perform marriages, the Laws of the United States must nevertheless prevail.   There are, after all, many in other 'professions' who may not be as well 'qualified' (less still be 'honest brokers') as all of us might wish they were - yet they also have the freedom to practice as such.

The author of this book realizes that it is likely to be purchased by many such ministers and that, whilst some may indeed be so educated and genuinely motivated as to be able to perform marriages, just as 'professionally' as those who have received all the necessary training for the clergy - there will be many others reading this book who, in all consciousness, should neither presume to consider themselves qualified, nor even attempt, to practice as a Minister of Religion, even if only to perform marriages.

If you are one of the latter;   consider carefully what you had in mind when you purchased this book.   Be honest with yourself - and not least of all with God - and **do not attempt** to be, or purport to be, what you know you are not.   If you were to try and, you 'mess up', you will not only bring trouble upon yourself - but even more importantly, you will almost certainly cause a lot of pain and heartache for others [e.g. the couples you 'married'] as well.

If you think you can 'fake it' by simply 'playing the part' as you may imagine from what you have observed of members of the clergy generally - don't fool yourself.   In no time at all, you will be asked questions [as a minister] which you'll be unable to answer adequately, and you'll quickly be 'found out' !   This book is certainly **not intended for you.**

The Development of the Christian Churches

I have been surprised to discover that many Ministers of Religion have little more than a vague knowledge (if that) of Christian denominations other than their own - less still of their origins !   Different denominations each have their own marriage rites which reflect their historical and theological origins.   Similarly, the majority of practising Christians seem to have little knowledge of the origins and tenets of other Christian religions, - including that of their spouses !

For your historical reference, **APPENDIX FOUR** to this book will provide you with a simplified 'Family Tree' showing the development of the Christian Churches, from what is commonly referred to as 'The Early Church'.

Following various early schisms and heresies, there was "The Great Schism" (1054) dividing the Church into Western and Eastern Churches - namely **The Church of Rome (Western)** on the one hand, and **The Orthodox (Eastern) Churches** [Russian, Greek, Syrian, Armenian and Coptic] on the other.

The Reformation in the 16th century brought about the division (in the West) away from the 'Roman Catholic' Church - to the 'Protestant' Churches, with subsequent divisions arising within the latter thereafter.

Later, in the United States, many other 'new groups' of Christian Churches evolved on their own - including such as: the Church of Jesus Christ of Latter Day Saints [Mormon];   the Seventh-Day Adventist Church;   the Church of Christ Scientist;   the Disciples of Christ, and other Churches of Christ along with the 'older' churches and societies brought over to America - some of which have since established their own independent hierarchy over here.

For example: Whereas a Roman Catholic bishop is nominated by His Holiness the Pope, and a Church of England bishop is nominated by the Sovereign [Her Majesty The Queen being the 'Defender of The Faith'] in the United States - and in some other episcopal churches elsewhere - a bishop is elected by the synod or diocesan parliament.

FOOTNOTE - 1993:

From time to time, one hears speculation in the media that Her Majesty Queen Elizabeth II, might abdicate in favour of her son, Prince Charles, so that he may become King before he is much older - bearing in mind that, by the time Queen Victoria died, her son and heir, who became King Edward VII, was somewhat advanced in years and reigned for such a short time.

Personally, I cannot envisage The Queen abdicating under any circumstances whatsoever.   She takes her duty and responsibility as "Defender of The Faith" [i.e. as Head of The Church of England] most seriously, and, it is a duty she has sworn to uphold until her death.   Her Majesty cannot simply 'resign' from that undertaking without breaking faith, and therefore will not do so.

She became Queen *automatically and immediately* upon the death of her father, King George VI. She subsequently took on the task and responsibility of "Defender of The Faith" upon being crowned at her Coronation in Westminster Abbey, in 1952.

On the other hand, King Edward VIII, who abdicated in favour of his younger brother, Prince Albert, who became King George VI in 1937 - was able to abdicate only because he had not yet been crowned, and thus had not yet taken on the responsibility also of being the "Defender of The Faith".   If he had taken on that responsibility by being actually *crowned* King, it would have been impossible for him (as by then also head of the church) to marry the twice *divorced* American woman, Wallace Simpson, and her becoming also "Queen" (consort).

Following his abdication, he was given the title (by which he is much better remembered) of H.R.H. The Duke of Windsor.   Upon her marriage to him, Wallace Simpson became "Duchess of Windsor" but, notably, *without* being allowed the prefix "H.R.H." [Her Royal Highness].

Hence all the questions arising now concerning the present separation - *but not any consideration of a divorce* - between Prince Charles, as heir to the Throne [and thus also sometime "Defender of The Faith"] and Princess Diana.   Whilst a member of the Church of England may get divorced, the Church will neither sanction nor condone divorce - and it could not therefore have at its head, sworn to "Defend The Faith", a divorcee.   Fortunately, the Church of England, being not quite so strict on the subject as the Church of Rome, does nevertheless acknowledge divorce, and allow divorcees to remain as members of the Church.

Incidentally, I would say that, when The Queen attended the marriage [in a small church in Scotland] of her divorced daughter, The Princess Royal [Princess Anne] to Commander Tim Laurence, Royal Navy;   she attended, *not* as The Queen, but privately as the mother of the bride.   Significantly, whilst other members of Anne's family attended, neither The Princess of Wales [Diana Spencer] nor The Duchess of York [Sarah Fergusson] were invited to attend !

PRE-MARRIAGE COUNSELLING ?

Whilst I personally insist upon meeting a couple and discussing their requirements with them in detail, as soon as possible after they have made a 'booking' with me for their Wedding - and in any case well in advance of their Wedding Day - I do not recommend that you should attempt to counsel them on all the intricacy of 'Marriage' and married life as such.   That is to say, not unless you are in fact suitably qualified and experienced as a Counsellor.   This is the job of their own priest, minister, or pastor - assuming that either or both of them are communicants in their own local church.

If they are not, then alternatively, it is to be hoped that their parents will have in any case helped to advise and guide them in such matters. Sadly, one all too often hears the confession "I'm not very religious" or "I believe in God, but I don't go to church...etc." and thus they are in any case reluctant to approach such as their local Parish Priest on the subject.   In some cases no doubt being afraid that they'll be in for a scolding from him, intent more upon getting them "back into the fold", than dealing with their immediate interest in being married !

In many instances also, it has in my experience been the case where, even a couple who do attend at church regularly, have decided that they would prefer to have their Wedding other than in church - because their own priest [especially if Roman Catholic] or pastor is going to insist upon their both first attending upon him for *"several weeks of counselling"* before he will even begin to firm up any specific arrangements to perform a marriage for them.

Frankly, I have met a lot of people who are regular church-goers, but who are anything but 'Christian' in their everyday lives - and a lot more who hardly ever go to church, who are nevertheless really very good Christians indeed.   Certainly 'good people' anyway.

There are many who do not know how to pray and who therefore have need to be led in prayer and, for that purpose, feel that this can only be achieved by attending a Church Service.   On the other hand, there are those who, for one reason or another, do not attend a church, often because they cannot understand, less still like, all the ceremony and ritual involved in so many of them.

> *To those folks, I have this to say: You do not have to go to church in order to "talk to God" - you can talk to Him anywhere at any time. And He will hear you.   He may not always respond immediately, nor in the manner you hope or expect of Him.   After all, He's a busy fellow and you're not the only one calling for His attention at that time ! But have faith and 'hang in there' talking to Him and, He will help you.   So don't feel that you have to be apologetic to me (just because I'm a priest) that you don't happen to go regularly to church. That's strictly a matter between you and the Almighty !*

Since you have probably been approached to officiate at their Wedding, as an 'independent' minister available to perform the marriage at some special venue of their choosing, your prime concern is with the Wedding itself - and not quite so much with their own preparation for marriage overall.

Thus, an interview is (in my view) essential, but not in-depth counselling as such.   My own interviews with couples prior to the Wedding usually take place in my own home, and last for up to about two hours at most.

The most important object of the interview is to ensure that the couple understand the precise meaning and portent of every word that they are going to be saying and/or answering to during their Marriage Service, and, that they not only understand the words, but honestly believe in them too.

More about this in the next chapter.

THE MINISTER'S INTERVIEW WITH THE BRIDAL COUPLE

The prime purpose of your meeting well beforehand with a couple for whom you are going to officiate in their Marriage Ceremony - quite apart from advising them on procedures and so forth - is to ensure that they have an 'Order of Service' for their Wedding, that is not only to their liking and appropriate for them, but one of which they fully comprehend its meaning and purpose.   Moreover, that they **believe what they themselves will be saying** during the Service.

For example: You don't not want to have anyone saying in their part of the Ring Ceremony: *"With this ring I thee wed,..............In the Name of the Father, and of the Son, and of the Holy Ghost, Amen."* if they do not understand the concept of, and believe in the Holy Trinity.

I have often had a bride and/or 'groom tell me that, whilst they believe in God and in Jesus Christ, they're "still not sure about the Holy Ghost" and maybe also cannot understand the concept of "God the Father, God the Son, God the Holy Ghost" as such, anyway.   Better in such cases to substitute such as: *"..........As God is my witness, Amen."*

The Order of Service for
The Solemnization of Holy Matrimony

There are of course many different forms of Service from which to choose, not least of all if you are a **'Non-Denominational Minister'** - for whom this book is primarily intended.   More of these various Services elsewhere in this book, but first let us consider the good old tried and true original or **'Traditional' Order of Service.**

Essentially, the same Marriage Vows have been spoken by most English-speaking couples for perhaps a thousand years and more.   The vows themselves have always been said in the mother tongue, but the Service as an whole was translated into English in the first Prayer Book, issued in 1549 under King Edward VI.   Only a few minor changes in the wording of the Marriage Service were made when the "Book of Common Prayer" was restored in 1662.

Most of the present-day denominational and individual marriage rituals are adaptions from this Traditional Service.   The full text set down elsewhere in this book, reproduces the traditional language (with modern punctuation) of the **essential parts** of the Service.

In many Catholic Churches, you will hear a quite different Service. However, this one is, in its simplified form, to the astonishment of many Catholics, so very familiar to them, many don't even notice the difference. It is really only when one *adds on to the 'basic service'* that one makes it a specifically 'Catholic' or 'Protestant' Service.

Thus, for couples where one party is a Catholic and the other is Protestant, this old 'Traditional' Service can serve equally well for both of them.

At this point, I feel it is appropriate for me to digress for a moment to deal with the misconception - held by many that the Roman Catholics are the **only** 'Catholics' - perpetuated for quite some time now by many of them being in the habit of 'dropping' the prefix "Roman".   Those of us in the Anglican Church are also 'Catholic' - as also are those in all other "Catholic and Apostolic" churches !

The Creed, as said in the Church of England for example, includes the words: **"And I believe one Catholick and Apostolick Church...etc."**

Moreover, it is equally correct to address an Anglican priest as "Father" - especially if he is 'High Church' - as it is customary to so address a priest of the Roman Catholic Church.   That is to say, not simply as "Reverend" - unless you are yourself neither Anglican nor Roman Catholic.

One 'difference' (between the 'Catholic' and 'Protestant' versions of the Marriage Service) is of course in the Lord's Prayer.   Whilst most of us 'Protestants' say "Our Father **which art** in heaven", Roman Catholics will say "Our Father **who art** in heaven";   and instead of "And forgive us our trespasses as we forgive **them that** trespass against us", Catholics will say "And forgive us our trespasses as we forgive **those who** trespass against us."

Also, whereas the Catholic version will end at: "But deliver us from evil." we invariably (but not always) continue *without a break*, with: "For thine is the kingdom, and the power, and the glory, for ever. Amen."   Catholics also include this latter part in The Mass, but with a break between this and the foregoing part.

You may ask: Why deal first with this old 'Traditional' Service ?   Well, as indicated above, it's the one from which most other Christian churches have taken guidance, and adapted to suit themselves - so where better to start ?   Personally, I don't think you can improve upon it anyway.

It "covers all the bases" and all too often, you'll find adaptations leaving out (or watering down) the most important parts in their effort to be different.   Endeavouring no doubt to also further distance themselves from the 'old' [Establishment's] often theatrical rituals - thoroughly enjoyed by many, but equally confusing and perplexing to many others.

You will frequently find that, after officiating at a Wedding using the 'Traditional' Service, you will have many of the guests - young as well as older - complimenting you on the Service, adding such remarks as *"How nice to hear the 'proper' Service again - I haven't heard it for years !"*

They have so often heard all sorts of 'Modern' or so-called 'Contemporary' Marriage Services - both in church and out - that they had almost forgotten about the 'original' until this occasion.   And they love it.   They find it refreshing and uplifting.   Even more importantly, **providing you read it slowly and clearly with due solemnity**, the words used do not fall upon deaf ears - they awaken (or re-awaken) their innermost belief in God.

The "Obey !"

This is such an important and, in today's Western Society such a controversial subject, that I shall deal with this separately in the next Chapter.

"And thereto I plight thee my troth"

Whilst going over the wording in the marriage service with the couple, you are quite likely to be asked what this means [in the man's vows] - simply, he is saying "and to all I have just promised, I pledge to you my fidelity" and similarly, from the woman she is saying "...I give to you my fidelity."

The Lesson

As you will know, the Order of Service for a Wedding, when held in a church or chapel can be very long, depending upon the denomination, the clergy officiating, and to some extent also the wishes of the couple themselves. In a Catholic Church, or in what may be referred to as 'High Church' Episcopal, it can last an extremely long time - and it is perhaps this factor alone that causes many of their parishioners to seek a venue (and also if necessary, an alternative member of clergy to officiate) for their wedding elsewhere.

This book being especially intended more for guidance of Non-Denominational Ministers and others officiating at Weddings "on neutral ground", one is concerned therefore with only what might well be described as the 'Short Form' - whilst nevertheless still offering all that is essentially required in The Solemnization of Holy Matrimony.

Thus, the 'Basic Simplified Service' lasting no more than about fifteen to twenty minutes at most - including the processional and recessional music - is preferable and, indeed, really all that is required.

The inclusion of a reading from the Holy Bible is certainly not essential. On the other hand, it is customary and, if both short and appropriate, most desirable. If the couple have any particular passage that is especially meaningful to both of them, you should of course give every possible consideration to their request and, if you find it appropriate, include it in the Service. In the absence of any such special request, you may care to put forward your own suggestions for their consideration.

One of the most appropriate for any Wedding is of course St. Paul's definition of love, real love - to be found in 1st Corinthians, Chapter 13, reading Verses 4 to 8 and 13. This only requires a very few moments and, read slowly and 'with emotion' can be highly rewarding for all who hear it. Since the reading is intended to be a 'Lesson', it should be read in such language as to be immediately and clearly understood by all to whom it is being read. I therefore recommend that, in preference to reading from the King James, you use (such as) "The New English Bible - New Testament" [1] in English that everyone can understand from the very first word you say.

The Prayers

Firstly, the Lord's Prayer. In the present day, there are to be heard several 'modern' variations of this [e.g. "Forgive us our debts...etc."] - none of which I am personally prepared to use. Whilst you'll have to use your own judgement as to which may be most acceptable to the couple you are

[1] OXFORD UNIVERSITY PRESS & CAMBRIDGE UNIVERSITY PRESS

interviewing, you can't go wrong if you keep to the original - which almost everyone attending will recognise and, hopefully, join with you in saying.

Sadly, although you as the Officiating Minister will say "Let *Us* Pray" - which means all of us present and not just you alone - all too often you'll find you're on your own, or, with only the Bride and 'Groom (and maybe their attendants also) joining in with you !   You may therefore care to change the invitation [command ?] to "Now let us all join together in saying the Lord's Prayer."

Following the Lord's Prayer, there should also be one more for you to add - which you'll find set down in the full text of the 'Traditional' Order of Service elsewhere in this book.

Prayer for Procreation of Children

Although not so often included the 'Order of Service' these days as in our parents' time and times before them, you may well wish to discuss with the couple - *unless "the woman is past child-bearing"* - whether or not they would like you to include prayers that they may both be "fruitful in procreation of children."   If, even in a 'simplified service' [i.e. short service] they do wish this, then these prayers should be inserted at some appropriate point in the service *after* they have made their vows and become 'man and wife.'

For example: In the old 'Traditional' Service (of the Anglican Church) you will find the following:

> *"O Merciful Lord, and heavenly Father, by whose gracious gift mankind is increased: We beseech thee, assist with thy blessing these two persons, that they may both be fruitful in procreation of children, and also live together so long in godly love and honesty, that they may see their children christianly and virtuously brought up, to thy praise and honour;   through Jesus Christ our Lord.   Amen.*

> *O God, who by thy mighty power hast made all things of nothing;   who also (after other things set in order) didst appoint, that out of man (created after thine own image and similitude) woman should take her beginning; and, knitting them together, didst teach that it should never be lawful to put asunder those whom thou by Matrimony hadst made one;   O God, who hast consecrated the state of Matrimony to such an excellent mystery, that in it is signified and represented the spiritual marriage and unity betwixt Christ and his Church: Look mercifully upon these thy servants, that both this man may love his wife, according to thy Word, (as Christ did love his spouse the Church, who gave himself for it, loving and cherishing it even as his own flesh,) and also that this woman may be loving and amiable, faithful and obedient to her husband;   and in all quietness, sobriety, and peace be a follower of holy and godly matrons.   O Lord, bless them both, and grant them to inherit thy everlasting kingdom;   through Jesus Christ our Lord,   Amen. "*

You need not of course use all of the above, nor for that matter, the words exactly as written - but take care how you compose any variations thereto !

The Benediction

In the ordinary course of events, you will invariably give the Blessing of the Holy Trinity [i. e. "God the Father, God the Son, God the Holy Ghost, bless, preserve, and keep you....."] to complete the Service.   However, in the event of the Bride and/or the 'Groom being unable to identify themselves with the Holy Trinity, whilst you may nevertheless suggest that 'it cannot hurt them' to be given the blessing of 'all three' - if they have a problem with this, you can of course modify this to instead read simply "God bless, preserve, and keep you;   the Lord mercifully with his favour look upon you.....etc."

'Holy Ghost' -vs- 'Holy Spirit'

You will occasionally have couples, especially if either or both parties are Catholic, requesting that you say "Holy Spirit" instead of "Holy Ghost".   This has been a matter of some debate for quite awhile now and it's really of no great consequence which you choose to say.

In most English Dictionaries, if you look up the word "Spirit", you will find the definition: "The Holy Ghost" !   Many latin scholars maintain that in translation from the Latin "Spiritus Sanctus" into English, one should say "Holy Ghost".   Others, seemingly more with Priests in the Holy Roman [Catholic] Church teach their flock to say "Holy Spirit" more often than "Holy Ghost" - perhaps because "Spirit" retains much the same 'ring' to the ear as the Latin "Spiritus" ?

Inter-Faith Services

In a marriage between Christians of two different denominations, inclusion of "of the Father, and of the Son, and of the Holy Ghost" [or Holy Spirit] will not ordinarily present any problems, nor of course "of our Lord Jesus Christ".   However, in a marriage between a Christian and a Jew, one has to avoid causing any offence to either party.

Where neither party has been divorced, they can of course have the full 'Inter-faith Service' - at which both a Priest and a Rabbi must officiate - which can be a very 'long-winded' affair and which most such couples prefer to avoid.   If either one of them has been married before [and Divorced not widowed] they are likely to be refused by Priest and/or Rabbi.

And, since you are, if a Non-Denominational Minister, not likely to become involved in any Inter-Faith Services, we need proceed no further (not in this book anyway) with any details on that subject.

Instead, let us consider the alternative of a Non-Denominational Service.

If the couple are of very different faiths, such as Christian and Buddhist, you will have much more of a problem in composing an appropriate Marriage Service for them.   With them you have **Almighty God** on the one hand and, the **Enlightened One** [i. e. Buddha] on the other.   Buddhism is an Asiatic religion - much older than Christianity - founded by Gautama Buddha in the 5th Century B. C.

Between a Christian and a Jew however, since both believe in one and the same God - no great problem.   You can even adapt the old 'Traditional' Marriage Ceremony of the Christian Church to suit, provided the couple both agree to this, by simply deleting all references to the Holy Trinity and to Jesus Christ - and retaining (or substituting) only the references to God.

On these occasions, I usually preface the proceedings with a very brief introduction much on the following lines:

> *Friends, we are gathered together here today in the sight of God, within the presence of this company, to join together this man and this woman in Holy Matrimony.   It is an honourable Estate, instituted by God, and symbolizing the concern of the whole community of mankind, in the Covenant which they are about to make.*
>
> *Before we proceed with the actual Service however, I would just like to say that, as a Chaplain (* and Minister of our Lord's Church), I am both honoured and most happy to be chosen as the instrument in uniting in marriage, two lovely people whose love for each other and whose common faith and belief in one and the same God, transcends the fact that one was brought up in the Jewish Faith and the other a Christian.*
> **We are all God's children !**

[* *this reference included only if the Jewish party has no objection.*]

Atheists and Agnostics

Atheism: [Def'] "Disbelief in *or denial of* the existence of God."

Agnostic: [Def'] "One who *doubts* the possibility of knowing the existence of God or absolute truth."

As a general rule, one will find that the Atheist is in effect "anti-God" in his (or her) posture on religion;   whereas the Agnostic will simply be a "non-believer" whilst at the same time finding no fault in and/or having no objections to anyone else around him (her) having belief and faith in God.

Thus far, to the best of my knowledge and belief, I have never performed a marriage between an Atheist and anyone else.   I have quite often however, performed a marriage between an Agnostic and a Christian or Jew, using a religious ceremony in so doing.

I still commence the service with "In the Name of the Father, and of the Son, and of the Holy Ghost.   Amen." - having (at interview beforehand) reminded the Agnostic party that I am saying this first for my own and everyone else's benefit and not asking him (or her) to say it, less still expecting him (or her) to make the Sign of the Cross at that moment !

In the Agnostic's vows, I shall of course **delete** the words **"according to God's holy ordinance"** and, in the Ring Ceremony, **substitute** simply **"as this company is my witness"** - but without changing anything for the other party.

As for the Blessing [Benediction] in such cases;   I remind the Agnostic that I am not asking him/her to say anything that he/she does not believe -

and I ask "do you really want to deny your wife/husband the Blessing of the Holy Trinity simply because you don't want it for yourself ?"   I then also explain that, my hope and belief is that, someday, he/she will be glad that he/she did receive that blessing upon them and their union.   Invariably, the Agnostic will appreciate the point and, agree to this, in which event I approach the giving of the Benediction, amending the final part of the Service to read as follows:

¶ *The Chaplain shall now address the Bride/Bridegroom asking her/him:*

_____, are you willing to join your Christian Husband (Wife) in receiving the Blessing of The Holy Trinity ?

¶ *Then, if the Bride ('Groom) shall reply:*

   I am.

¶ *Then the Chaplain shall add **this** Blessing,*

God the Father, God the Son, God the Holy Ghost, Bless, preserve, and keep you;   the Lord mercifully with His favour look upon you, and so fill you with all spiritual benediction and grace, that you may so live together in this life, that in the world to come, you may have life everlasting.   AMEN.

Following which, I then make the Presentation: "Ladies and gentlemen, I now have the honour to present to you Mr. & Mrs. ...."

Frankly, I do not (unless specifically requested beforehand so to do) add the words "You may now kiss the bride."   As far as I'm concerned, that is for Hollywood [i.e. Films and Television] and, he certainly doesn't need my permission to kiss her !   You'll usually find that, the moment you have presented them to the assembled company, they will automatically embrace – before you have time to invite him to kiss her.   However, should there be any hesitation on his part and, the Recessional Music perhaps having not yet commenced, I might look at him and say: "And you don't need my permission.......!"

Incidentally, if the Marriage is performed in a Church or Chapel, I would neither 'Present' them, nor invite the 'groom to kiss his bride, anyway.

Other Arrangements

There will probably be many other matters to discuss with the couple at interview as well.   The Marriage Licence;   who will be 'giving the Bride away' [Father or friend, etc.];   the attendants - Maid (or Matron) of Honour, Bridesmaids, Bridegroom's Supporter [i.e. Best Man], 'Groomsmen and Ushers, Ring Bearer (if any) and Flower Girls (if any) and the order of processional.

Also such matters as how they (and their attendants) will be dressed and, *if you are entitled to wear naval or military uniform* (as an alternative to clerical dress or plain civilian dress), what they would prefer to have you wear.   Have they arranged for a photographer, video, decorations, etc.

If they have not already done so;   where and when to obtain the necessary Marriage Licence.   In California, which type to get;   if they are already living together and not aware of the 'Confidential Licence', you should tell them about it.

Concerning who is to 'give the Bride away'.   The Prayer Book states that "the priest receives the bride *at the hands of her father or friend.*" Thus if the bride's father is not available, then since *"or friend"* does not indicate gender, it does not have to be a man.   The bride's mother can and is often both surprised, and delighted, to hear that she can have that honour.

If neither father nor mother are available, and the honour is given to a friend to escort the bride to her Wedding, I often change the wording from "Who *giveth* this woman to be married to this man ?" to instead read "Who *presenteth* this woman to be married to this man ?"

In responding, whereas the father (or whomsoever) would normally say simply "I do" - if both father and mother are present, I suggest beforehand to him that it would be much nicer if he cares to respond: "Her mother and I do." I have had occasions where the bride's father is not long deceased, and her mother has chosen to reply: "Her father in spirit, and I do."

Where a bride has been married before;   whether now a widow or divorced and sometimes suggesting that, since her father had already 'given her away' once, he could not do so again - to this I respond "why not ?"   In either case [death or annulment] presumably she subsequently, whether physically or only in being, returned to the bosom of her parents.   And so frankly, I can see no impediment in the bride having her father 'give her away' again.

I certainly do not like to see a bride having to approach the Altar [or other designated place for the marriage] walking unescorted.   Surely there must be *someone* who would appreciate the honour of escorting her to this most important event in her life ?

Where there is *not* to be a Ring Bearer;   then it is customary for the 'Best Man' to hold the Wedding Ring that the 'groom is going to give to his bride and for the 'Maid of Honour' [if married, 'Matron of Honour'] to hold the Second Ring (if any) that the bride is going to give to her bridegroom.   In each case, it is you as the Officiating Minister, who will "receive the ring(s)" from the 'Best Man' and 'Maid of Honour' respectively to then hand to the 'groom and bride, in each case at the appropriate moments in the course of the service.

Wedding Co-ordinators

At many venues [e.g. Hotels, Restaurants, etc.] you will find that there is a 'Wedding Co-ordinator' who has been engaged by the bride and 'groom - or whomsoever is paying for the Wedding and/or Reception - to "make all the arrangements" for them.

All too often some of these wedding co-ordinators take it upon themselves to also coach the bride and 'groom on precisely who follows whom in the processional, and who stands where to do what and when during the service -

*without any prior reference to, or consultation with, the minister who is
to perform the marriage !* Frequently you will find that these people have
their own ideas of what is or is not supposedly "correct for the present
day", and, that their ideas may be in conflict with yours.

Whenever there is any possibility of a 'Wedding Co-ordinator' being in any
way involved in the proceedings - make a point of making contact with him
(or more often her) immediately upon your arrival.   You should in any case
as a matter course, always arrive at least half-an-hour in advance of the
time prescribed for the marriage to commence - if only to (i) receive into
your hands and check the Marriage Licence and (ii) provide a final briefing
to both the Bride and her entourage, and the Bridegroom and his supporters
in the ceremony.

The arrangements for catering, seating, decorations and so forth are of
course very much the responsibility of the Wedding Co-ordinator.   However,
insofar as the 'Order of Service' (which must include the Processional) is
concerned, it must remain the prerogative of the Minister to prevail over
any intrusion by the Wedding Co-ordinator into any part of the proceedings
that is his domain.

Personally, I cannot and will not tolerate interference from such Wedding
Co-ordinators who say to couples "we always do it this way here" and who
think that they know as much, or more, about marriage services and
procedures than does the clergy.   I would not presume to tell them how to
do their job - and they should not presume to interfere in mine.

This said, there are nevertheless many Wedding Co-ordinators who DO show
due respect and consideration for the clergy, and who will make a point of
asking a couple whom is to perform the marriage - and where they can get
into touch with the minister, so that they can *properly co-ordinate* their
respective duties and responsibilities.

If you find for example, that;   some so-called 'Wedding Co-ordinator' has
taken the liberty of presuming to tell the bride that she and her father
are to proceed in a certain manner, and this is contrary to what you
require and had previously agreed upon with the couple, you are to correct
this immediately - and if necessary, maybe also (politely) tell the co-
ordinator to "mind their own business !"   Similarly, if the co-ordinator
has told the bridegroom that he is to 'receive' his bride immediately upon
her arrival at the 'altar', rather than remain apart until after the
minister has first "received the bride from her father....etc.", then you
must also correct this situation without delay.   Otherwise, the whole
ceremony could result in a fiasco.

Vestments

In almost all cases, whenever you are performing a marriage "on neutral
ground" you should *not* (nor will you be expected to) wear 'Full Vestments'.

Unless in Naval or Military (Chaplain's) Uniform, it should suffice for you
to wear ordinary Clerical Dress with Surplice [i.e. The loose white linen
vestment worn by officiating clergy and choristers] and Stole [i.e. a Vest-

ment consisting of a long strip with ends hanging down in front from back of neck - usually with an embroidered Cross at each end.]

Bride's Wedding Dress

If the marriage is to take place aboard such as a motor yacht (or any other relatively small vessel at sea), I strongly recommend that the Bride shall be well advised **NOT** to wear a dress that has a long 'train' to it, nor even a dress that actually touches the deck.   Strictly speaking a 'train' is: "A trailing prolongation of a robe or gown."   Without a doubt, if it has a long train, she will not be leaving that vessel without having had someone stand on it, and it will be damaged.   And, even if her dress only slightly 'drags' along the deck, it will probably become dirtied.

Exceptionally, if the dress is with a 'train';   whilst the bride may trail her dress during the Processional, she should not make a Recessional with her husband upon conclusion of the marriage service, unless it is such that she can gather it up and 'carry' it over her arm, or alternatively, she can first have her Maid [or Matron] of Honour immediately pin it up on to small hooks with loops built into the design for this purpose - before she moves a step away from where the marriage took place.

Some trains are in fact designed to be simply and quickly removed entirely; and the Maid/Matron of Honour can achieve this in a matter of moments for the bride.   Elsewhere, a full flowing Bridal Gown may be just fine - and even then it may well be advisable to "do something about the train" before reaching the Reception - but in confined quarters, such as aboard any small vessel at sea;   definitely not !

I recall an occasion awhile ago aboard a large private yacht [a small ship really] where the couple had forgotten to bring the licence, so I sent the 'Best Man' home for it.   It only took him forty-five minutes to return with the licence but, while he was away and we waited at the dock, they opened the Bar.   In their anxiety and, to pass the time, having also as yet had nothing to eat, all were drinking far too much.

By the time the 'Best Man' returned, he and I found that, apart from the Captain and crew, we were just about the only totally sober folks on board.   Most of the others were very 'merry' indeed - including the bride and 'groom !   At one point (since we had a six hours cruise at sea ahead of us anyway), I almost decided to postpone the marriage until later but, in the event, fearing that they might meanwhile imbibe even more, I decided to proceed as planned.

The bride was wearing what I must presume to have been a hired dress that had, perhaps, been frequently cleaned and in the process weakened the seams.   It was a truly superb gown, with a very long train to it. After the marriage, the bride caught sight of an old friend standing several yards away over at the other side of the ship and, in her excitement (and 'merry' state) moved off at speed towards that person.

She had not noticed that her father was standing on the train of her dress at the time;   nor did she feel anything when, the train and back panel (which ran all the way up both sides to her waist) simply ripped away.   She wasn't wearing a slip - so all one could see (or happened to observe) was a pair of white panties going off into the distance ! Cameras flashed - and the Video man promptly went to 'zoom lense' !

The moral of this story:

   (i)   Don't forget to bring the Marriage Licence with you;

   (ii)   When in crowded quarters, don't wear a Wedding Dress with a long
          train to it, and

   (iii) Don't open the bar before the Service !

Formal or Semi-Formal ?

Not only does the degree of formality a couple desire for their wedding determine the appropriate clothing for them - and everyone else in the 'Wedding Party' - but also the time of day for the marriage ceremony.

If it is to be after 6 o'clock, it's considered an evening event, but if to be earlier, then it's definitely a daytime event.   A simple, elegant style of dress is always in good taste at any hour - but evening celebrations permit more elaborate attire.

All of the men in the 'Wedding Party' should be dressed in *identical* formal (or semi-formal) attire - especially the fathers who should 'match' that of the bridegroom and his supporters - the only exceptions to this rule being if any of them [e.g. Bridegroom and 'Best Man'] may be in Naval or Military uniform, and the other men may not, or any man who is a Clergyman used to wearing a clerical collar.

Both the bride's mother and the bridegroom's mother should, ideally, wear dresses that complement each other - both in style and colour.

Wedding Invitations

You may well be asked by couples to advise them on the correct wording for the Invitations.   This can vary considerably depending on circumstances vis-a-vis who is to make the invitations and, whether the marriage is to be performed in church, at the home of friends, or a military wedding; if it is a second marriage for the bride; if a widowed parent is the host; if the bride's remarried mother is the host; if the bride's remarried father is the host - or if the couple themselves are the hosts - and so on !

Space here does not permit me to give examples of all the alternatives so I recommend that, if you are not already well versed in this subject, you get into touch with a good printer-engraver who specialises in Wedding Invitations - and obtain a full set of specimen printings for your future reference.

Do *not* rely upon simply collecting invitations sent to you by couples whom you have previously married - theirs might not all be correct.   Indeed, it is more than likely that most will not !

Processional and Recessional Music

There is of course much from which to choose.   Bearing in mind that the much used (although strictly inappropriate) traditional Wedding Marches by Wagner and Mendelssohn continue in popularity and are frequently requested, I always carry with me *in case of need,* audio cassettes of these as part of my 'kit'.   They are really inappropriate since the "Here Comes the Bride" chorus from Wagner's *"Lohengrin"* - occurs in the opera when the bride and 'groom enter the bridal chamber, and before the act is over, the 'groom has murdered a rival and has to abandon his wife forever.   And the Mendelssohn music was composed for Shakespaer's *"A Midsummer Night's Dream"* centred on a workman named Bottom, who is transformed into a jackal and courts and bewitches a fairy - in a musical fantasy filled with sensuality and magic !

Nevertheless, 'grand' sounding music that you'll be hard pushed to persuade those who want it, from using it.

Wedding Videos

I have built up a small 'library' of excellent videos of "my weddings" over recent years - all being extracts from professionally made full-length recordings - copied on to separate VHS cassettes for different 'Orders of Service' and/or at different venues.   Thus, I can select a particular cassette that will have on it extracts from several Weddings, all of which were performed at the same venue [so that the couple can see exactly how and where their marriage will take place] each Wedding on that cassette with minor variations of the same [e.g. Traditional] Service.

> *Many of "my weddings" are performed at sea aboard private charter vessels, where limited space and the configuration of the vessel requires that much of the traditional procedures such as the seating of the guests cannot be followed and, the Processional and Recessional has to be considerably modified.   Viewing beforehand, a video of how you arrange everything and, how and where you perform a marriage aboard any particular vessel, will greatly assist you in your briefing of the couple at interview.*

If you do not already have any suitable videos, or even extract copies of any of the Weddings you have performed, I strongly recommend that you start getting some together as soon as you can.   You will find them extremely helpful at interviews with couples.   They will return home a lot less 'anxious' about what is ahead of them in the ceremony etc., having seen how you perform the marriage.   It also enables you to 'pause' the tape at each and every stage where either you may have a special point to make, or they have a question for you concerning any part of the proceedings.

TO "OBEY" ?

In the present-day climate of the 'Equality of the Sexes', you do not have to be a chauvinist to observe that in many situations, it is difficult to follow "traditional" ways and forms without it being misunderstood.   In part, this arises due to lack of opportunity to explain the meaning of the traditional form of the Order of Service.   The interview is the ideal time to review with the bridal couple, the proper and practical meaning of the word "obey" in the traditional Order of Service.

In dealing with the matter of the word "obey", the problem is largely one of semantics and what the word conjures up in the mind - imagining that it is used as in the military.   In short, interpreting this as an undertaking to be subservient to, and to at all times immediately and without question, comply with, every 'command' of the husband !   Having been schooled (or more accurately, misinformed) in this belief, it is not surprising that so many women, upon being asked if they wish to have "the obey" remain in the Service, will quickly reply "No way" - or in other words to that effect !

If you simply leave it at that, *you are doing both the Bride and the 'Groom a terrible disservice.*   The matter needs to be explained, quietly, and at some length - if possible, with the injection of a little humour as well. What follows now is how one may well best deal with this 'problem' - addressing the couple together at interview:

(1)   Frankly, I do not believe that God intended or requires that the wife should do, or agree with, *everything* that her husband asks her to do. The 'obey' *does not* invest in him the authority of a Sergeant-Major as over a Private in the Army.   If he has any sense, he will probably do what she asks him to do most of the time anyway.

(2)   Most of your vows are exactly the same.   "For better for worse, for richer for poorer, in sickness and in health.....etc." - *except one !* And that is *a major undertaking from the man*, which is made separately in the Ring Ceremony, when he says "With this ring I thee wed, *with my body I thee worship, and with all my worldly goods I thee endow*: in the name of the Father.....etc."   What he is really saying is this:

> "From this day forth, I don't just give you may name; *I take you completely into my care and protection, to be responsible for you - with all that I can physically do for you* [with my body I thee worship] *and with all that I have and can provide for you* [with all my worldly goods I thee endow].   In short, what was mine, is no longer mine;   it's ours;   and when I'm 'gone' it's all yours."

It has been that way for hundreds of years, because most of us men are not only the prime 'bread-winners' in the family, but also usually seem to 'kick the bucket' long before our wives.

Incidentally, just in case you may wonder about the husband promising to "worship" his wife;   the word actually means "serve".   Thus, for example: When you worship [pray to] God, you are serving God - and so likewise, the husband promises that (physically) he will do all he can to serve [support, care for, and defend] his wife.

Many years ago, when the husband died (unless there was a male heir to become head of the house) no one questioned for a moment that their home and everything in it, was now the property of his widow - he had endowed it to her on their Wedding Day.   What present-day California Lawyers would make of that may be another matter - but we're talking here about "God's Ordinance";   not those laid down by mere mortals.

Indeed, as I might say to the 'groom: "From that day forward - she's your problem !", which remark invariably serves not only to bring a little humour into the conversation, but also to make it very clear to both of them just how much of a commitment this is for him.

(3)   One may continue to further drive home to both of them, the portent of all this, by quoting as an example of the husband's heavy responsib- ilities, the following:

> At the start of your marriage, you may both be working, bringing two sources of income into the home.   Later you have a child. Perhaps your wife will be like many young women these days and, after a few weeks, feeling perfectly fit again, will arrange to 'park' your baby in a Day Care Centre - and promptly return to work.
>
> Alternatively, she might well decide [or at least desire] instead to stay at home for (say) the next four years, and be a full-time mother bringing up your child until he (or she) is ready to start at school.   Suddenly, one income for the house has stopped for awhile - then it's... "your problem Dad."

Of course, family economics may determine otherwise and, this obviously cannot be an arbitrary decision of the wife alone - but the responsibility remains the same and, 'Dad' should try to plan ahead accordingly, to meet this possible eventuality if he can.

(4)   In return, when the Bride vows "to love, cherish, and to obey", she is really saying: *"I not only love this man, I trust this man, I put my life in his hands, to take care of me (and our children) and so, where he goes, I go.*   If we cannot agree upon some major issue that is going to affect our whole family - or even just the two of us - where a decision has got to be made;   I have decided before we go into this that, we are not going to argue and 'fight' over the matter like so many other couples do - and end up in Divorce.   I'll let him decide what is best for all of us, and abide by his decision."

There may be many things in life upon which a couple don't happen to agree;   unimportant little things on which they can 'agree to disagree'. However, sooner or later some question will arise, upon which they don't agree, but on which a decision has to be made.   The matter affects them both and making a decision cannot be avoided.

> For example: Let us say that the husband is offered a 'super job' several hundred miles away in another State.   He may or may not particularly fancy moving there, but nevertheless feels that, having weighed up all the pro's and con's (and discussed the matter

thoroughly with his wife) it really would be best for all concerned, for him to accept the offer. Now his wife's immediate reaction to this may be simply "I want us to stay here; I like it here; all my friends are here; my mother lives nearby and can 'baby-sit' for us, etc.," or even ... "We're not going!"

Thus, *an impasse*, deadlock, dilemma - all the makings of a fight if someone does not 'keep their cool' and look again at the 'bottom line'. What are you going to do? If one of you tries to *impose* your will upon the other, and force the issue to one's own preference - sooner or later *resentment* will creep into your marriage and, it will grow, and grow, and grow.

Most things in life are designed to *avoid an impasse*. We all agree to abide by the majority vote - even if it required a "casting vote" by the Chairman of a Committee (or whatever) to decide an issue. In marriage [if the 'traditional' vows and undertakings remain unchanged] the *ultimate responsibility* for the well-being of the whole unit is vested in the husband. It is on his shoulders where (as the late Harry Truman put it) "the buck stops here." And along with that responsibility he should therefore also have the "casting vote" - to exercise if and when absolutely necessary. It is of course of paramount importance that, every husband should both understand and accept *the limitations of that privilege* - and only exercise it as and when he is certain that it really is in the best interests of the family [and not his personal interests alone] for him so to do.

In times past, some husbands assumed unto themselves a totalitarian power and authority over their wives and all within their domain. They 'possess' rather than love their wives and children. There are even today, some men who still do so - insecure men - who will behave in that manner whether or not their wives have vowed to 'obey' them. And, sadly, there will always be women who are in awe of such men, and who subsequently will be foolish enough to marry them.

One can most appropriately liken the marriage 'chain of command' to the relationship between the Captain of a ship and, his fellow officers and crew. One cannot run a ship by committee - someone has to decide which way to go, especially if approaching a storm. The Captain may seek the professional advice of such as his Navigating Officer and the Chief Engineer, whilst weighing up his options - but it will be the Captain who will decide, when, at what speed, and on what course the ship is to proceed.

Being ultimately responsible for the safety of his ship, and all who sail in her, the decision must be his. No ship could make it through an hurricane if it had two captains - and those two captains were to spend their time arguing about what should be done!

In the home, the husband must be both the 'Captain and Navigator' with the wife serving as the 'Mate' or Executive Officer - and probably 'Chief Engineer' too - upon whom every Captain is highly dependent anyway. As the children grow older, they too will all have their respective responsibilities to assume, and duties to perform within the family - as the 'Crew'.

(5) You should not be going into marriage with even the faintest thought in the back of your mind that, if it doesn't work out, you can get divorced.

Think about it;   this is to be "till death us do part" and "according to God's holy ordinance."   If the man is not *100% certain* in his own mind that he can answer truthfully "I will" to the question *"and forsaking all others, keep thee only unto her, so long as ye both shall live ?"* and likewise the woman also, to the same question - they should not be getting married.

And if the woman is not *100% certain,* that she not only loves the man, but can also feel sufficiently confident of his love *to 'trust him* and put her life in his hands' - and so pledge "to love, cherish, and [if necessary] to obey" him - *she probably has the wrong man.*

If any couple cannot feel sufficiently confident of each other's implacable love, and total commitment to one another, to make the traditional vows - yet despite this, still wish for one reason or another, to be legally married - then for them it *might* be better that they have only a Secular Ceremony and be married only in the eyes of the State, and not also of God.

Having said this, there is nevertheless still a case for those who, despite feeling unable to accept the 'Traditional' service in its original form - being at least honest with themselves and not wanting to be hypocritical in their vows - they still wish to have a religious service and be married also "before God and this company."

It may be that, *their present thinking* is that "if and when" some major problem arises, and "if" they cannot then agree upon the right decision to make, they'll simply have to "cross that bridge when they come to it" - then albeit (in my view) running the risk of an impasse, but hopefully being by then able to see the wisdom of the "obey", it is of course still preferable that they be married "before God" and not simply married only in the eyes of the State.

If either party is not entirely happy about it and wishes to have his or her part deleted after all [i.e. in the Ring Ceremony from the man, or the 'obey' from the woman] - *then you must delete both parts.*   One cannot have one without the other.   In short, you'll be giving them what some now refer to as the 'Modern Version' of the otherwise 'Traditional' Service.

In any event, all couples should be told: "Don't make vows 'before God' that you do not sincerely and wholeheartedly intend to keep."

A friend of mine told me about a Wedding at which he was a guest, where, in the Marriage Service, he heard the couple's vows include *"for so long as our love shall last"* [i.e. substituted for "so long as we both shall live"] at which just about everyone present was, quite rightly, absolutely astonished.

This is what can happen when some couples are left to write their own !

It will sometimes be the case where, both the 'Groom being fully prepared to give his Bride the undertaking required of him in the Ring Ceremony, and the Bride being equally prepared to make her's with the 'obey' - they nevertheless have a problem with the modern connotation of the word itself. Often it's simply no more than worrying about what some of their (uninformed) guests are going to make of it after the ceremony - and not wanting a 'hassle' from them spoiling their day, even if only in fun. More often than not however, if you remind them that "it's your wedding, not theirs" they'll stay with the original wording.

On the other hand, if employing the word "obey" really does present a problem, there is of course always *an alternative way* - of making precisely the same pledge.

> **For example:** instead of the bride saying "to love, cherish, and to obey" - how about her saying *"to love, cherish, and be loyal unto thee"* ? It matters only that the bride means this to be the same, and that God knows she means the same. And if any of their guests who are listening for the 'obey' don't hear it, and this alternative goes right 'over their heads', then that's not for the couple to worry about !

You will invariably find that, once a couple have these most important undertakings put into their proper perspective in this way, they will not only realise why they have been included in the 'Traditional' Order of Service - and stood the test of time for so many hundreds of years - they will choose to have you keep them in the Service.

One final, and hopefully convincing word about the benefits (for the couple) of using the 'original' version of the Traditional Order of Service. Whilst I have seldom, if ever, heard anyone among the guests snicker or make any remarks at all (during the service) upon hearing the bride say the word "obey" in her vows - I have from time to time had one or two women approach me after the service saying something to the effect "How did you get her to say that ?"

I first reply that I did not 'get her' to say that - she herself chose so to do. And I then go on to give the same explanation, as I had earlier given to the bride and 'groom, as to precisely what it all means, and that it does not mean what so many other women have come to **assume** is meant by 'obey' - in this context anyway. Invariably, I'll find that this results even in some 'feminist', albeit begrudgingly, saying "Now I come to think about it, that's not a bad deal !", and other ladies present saying "I wish I had had the 'obey' in the service when I got married."

It was one such young lady who came to me after a Wedding some time ago, whom I quote as a rather *sad, but very good example* of why the 'obey' (and the husband's major undertaking also) is in the original version, and why it has proved so practical and sensible to adhere to for all those hundreds of years. When I asked her why she now wished that she had promised to 'obey', she replied quietly, and sadly as follows:

> *"About eighteen months ago, my husband was offered a really wonderful new job in Miami, Florida. My immediate reaction to this, as my mind conjured up visions of 'hurricanes*

*and floods' was;   No way, we're not going;   we're staying right here in California.
My husband and I argued and argued for hours, losing our tempers, saying such terrible
things to each other that neither of us would retract - to the point where he finally
walked out of the house, didn't come back and, like so many others in similar
situations, we subsequently got divorced.*

*We're still in touch now because of our child.   We find that we still love each other
deeply after all - but it's too late now !   On the 'rebound' immediately after our
divorce, he married someone else.   Now he has that wonderful job in Florida but is
very unhappy in a marriage that should never have happened - and I'm unhappy here in
California on my own with our four-years old son, who is also unhappy.*

*I'm a woman who keeps her word and, if I had promised to 'obey' [knowing what I know
now about it's purpose in the marriage], while I might have said it 'through my teeth'
as I was feeling about it at the time, I would have said - alright, if you think it's
best for us to move to Florida, so be it.   Looking back now, I do so wish I had;   we
would still be together as a family and, all still be happy together."*

A sad reflection on our 'modern' society wherein it seems that far too many
of us forget that there can be much more pleasure in the giving, than in
receiving.   We have been so conditioned to 'look out for number one' to
the extent that we give less and less thought and consideration for
everyone else.   Often without realizing that, in the end, those whom we
hurt most, may indeed be ourselves and those closest to us !

What if the woman earns more than the man ?

In some marriages, it will transpire that the wife is earning more than her
husband - and it may be that she is also the better educated and qualified
of the two of them.   This often gives rise to the question: "So why should
the man make the 'final major decisions' for them ?"

To say that his is the 'traditional role' of father, hunter, bread-winner,
and defender of the family unit, etc.   Will that reply satisfy the woman
who will ask such a question ?   I doubt it.   It all depends entirely upon
how the woman looks upon her man, not only as a man, but as her prospective
partner and mate - for life !

There may well come a time, indeed probably will come a time, when she can
no longer work for awhile, or no longer be earning more than he can - in
which event, he will then become at least the major if not sole provider,
for his wife and family.

This is a question that can only be left to the couple to decide upon for
themselves - so long as it's not later, but *before* they get married.

I had a case sometime ago, where, it so happened that the woman was at
that time earning much more than the man.   He was a young Attorney at
Law, just starting out in his profession; she was a Doctor of Medicine
who had already become well-established as a specialist in her own
special field of surgery.

She nevertheless chose to have the "obey" in their marriage, and he in
his turn, to give the full original undertaking to her when giving her

the Wedding Ring.   Their reasoning ?   Quite apart from her wanting, albeit not as yet, to have children - and when then so blessed, intending to remain at home with them at least during their early years - her even more importantly wanting to look upon him as *"her own and her children's protector and ultimate provider"* in their home.

They had carefully made plans for their future.   She would continue in her profession whilst he got himself better established in his - and meanwhile not to have children until, (i) their combined incomes built the home they wanted for a family, and (ii) he could then subsequently afford to properly support a family.

Asked if, given that her husband might later have an opportunity to better himself in a Law Office elsewhere - which would necessitate their moving, and her thus having to quit her own presently most lucrative (and satisfying) position; what then ?   She replied without hesitation: "Go with my husband and, if we're not yet ready to start having a family; accept whatever position I can obtain as a Doctor, near to our new home."

As for any couple that require a 'Pre-Nuptial Agreement' to be entered into [i.e. under Civil Law] between them, before being married - whether it be because of his existing wealth or hers - allowing for the possibility of failure in their marriage and a subsequent divorce.   This always has me wondering about his or her motivation for this and, if they should really get married at all.   That is to say, unless only in a **Secular Ceremony.**

How can anyone go into marriage, prepared on the one hand to make vows *"before God"* which include the words *"until death us do part"* - knowing at the same time, that there have been preconditions set down and agreed upon, allowing for (*or perhaps even anticipating*) the possibility of a divorce ? One might just as well say: "Let's live together (*as if* we were husband and wife) and see how it works out !"

If either party cannot wholeheartedly and, without any reservations whatso-ever, *trust* as well as love the other - then one is bound to wonder about his or her motivation for the marriage in the first place.

The reader will by now have probably gained the impression that I am intent upon actually 'persuading' everyone I can to have the Traditional Service, in its 'original version' - and that all women should 'obey' their husbands at all times, whether they want to or not.   **Not so.**   I am however intent upon both men and women understanding and appreciating its benefits (and limitations) so that none shall miss the opportunity of having such a service, simply by default of a minister explaining and offering it to them.

Too often, one hears all sorts of 'fashionable' marriage services churned out by clergymen pandering to the whims of those who say "please keep it simple - we don't want anything *too* religious."   To such couples, one must ask if they really want to make any really lasting and meaningful promises "before God" to one another at all ?   Marriage is a very serious matter indeed, and far too few couples (young and old alike) take it as seriously as they should.

I have had many, many couples come to me for interview, for whom it was not until after I had taken them step-by-step through the entire (traditional) service - which really does cover "all the bases" - that for the first time they then began to realize what marriage means.

I have occasionally had couples who have been living together for some time, arrive for interview wanting "to get married" - and leave having decided that they should not do so after all.

I have told them to contact me again IF and when they find they don't just want to live and sleep together as *at present*, but really to 'share every-thing, good and bad, *for life'*.   A few have returned some months later to say "now we're sure", while most others have called me on the 'phone within a day or two to thank me for "opening their eyes in time", adding that they're now going to go their own separate ways.

Read again: I Corinthians, 13: 4-8, 13.

FOOTNOTE

Depending upon the way things are going between the bridal couple and your-self during the interview, and if you find that they are among those who now wish for the return of the best in 'traditional standards' you may - *in your own discretion* - care to read from (or even give them a copy of) my 'Epilogue' to this book.

It's quite surprising how many couples comment on "how things have changed" and "not in all respects for the better" - in the way that men and women now generally tend to view each other most of the time.

"UNISEX" VERSIONS ?

Converting to "Unisex" Wording in The Service !

Although I have only been asked *by less than 0.25%* [i.e. less than one in every four hundred] of the couples who have come to me over many years to have me marry them - to change every mention of "man" to "people" and such as "mankind" to "humankind" and so forth - I feel that this is nevertheless a topic which cannot be overlooked, especially by the readership for whom this book is intended.

One or two [Brides] have even had the temerity, to request that an actual reading from *The Bible* be 'amended' to better please and suit *them* in *their* determination to have everything fall within *their* conception of what is required for "equality" in marriage ! The Bridegroom in each case, I must presume, being too weak or too frightened to 'rock the boat' at this stage by pointing out to his fiancee the errors in her reasoning for this.

For example: St. Paul's definition of real 'love' as is set down in First Corinthians 13: 4-13. where he says *"Love keeps no score of wrongs; does not gloat over other men's sins, but delights in the truth"* - requesting that I should delete *"men's sins"* and substitute *"others' sins"* ! Speaking for myself, and no doubt also for the vast majority of other priests, under no circumstances whatsoever would I agree to such a request.

Similarly, in the centuries-old traditional 'Order of Service' one simply cannot change (in the preamble, for example) quoting St. Paul as having *"commended [marriage] to be honourable among all men"* to instead read: *"all persons."* And, (also in demanding of among the congregation) *"If any man can show just cause ..... let him now speak, or else hereafter forever hold his peace."* - to change this to such as *"person"* and *"their"* (or whatever) would in my view be simply pandering to the *'fetish'* (or maybe ignorance) of the individual making such a request.

Not least of all in the Prayers, where we pray *"O Eternal God, Creator and Preserver of all mankind..."* I am not about to change all such references in either The Bible or The Prayer Book to read *"humankind"* instead - not least of all, not to have other **mature** members of the congregation imagine that I don't know that "mankind" means "all of humankind" anyway.

Any good English Dictionary defines the word *"man"* firstly as *"Human being, person, one, the human race"* - and similarly, *"mankind"* as referring to *"the human species"* - as any reasonably well-educated individual should know. If one looks up the word *"humankind"* one finds firstly *"Of man - as opposed to other animals."* Accordingly, I can see no merit whatsoever in any request to discard the time-honoured and *correct language* of our Lord's Church.

Sadly, these are facts that are misunderstood by the more 'blinkered feminists' who insist upon accentuating and thus encouraging division ["us and them"] instead of true unification and mutual respect between men and women - by presuming a right to substitute such **misnomers** (as in this particular context they certainly are) as "persons" and "humankind" [for "man" and "mankind"] at every possible opportunity - in their attempts to produce some sort of 'Unisex' version, of everything !

I am just waiting for one of them someday, to really show how illogical she is being - by perhaps also wanting us to somehow change "Our Father" in the Lord's Prayer !   Incidentally, I have already seen car bumper-stickers referring to God as female.   This, even if intended to be humourous - is in my view, in exceptionally bad taste and an insult not only to Him, but also to one's intelligence.

All to often, such misguided (albeit sincere and well-intentioned) *fetishism* by these women eventually proves to be *counter-productive* to the 'cause' of equality for women anyway.   As Shakspere put it: *"Methinks thou protesteth too much !"*

For my further remarks on this subject, I refer you to the **"EPILOGUE"** in this book - located immediately before the several Appendices.

The "Obey" ?

This has certainly become an 'optional' item in deference to the movement toward "equality of the sexes" and is dealt with at some length - defined in an understandable and, I pray, correct context - in **the previous chapter** of this book.

THE 'TRADITIONAL' ORDER OF SERVICE
[ORIGINAL VERSION]

The Order for Marriage following in this chapter is set down in its most simplified yet still 'original' form, including the 'obey' in the woman's vows and, the major undertaking given in the Ring Ceremony by the man.

Immediately following it, is set down a slightly fuller version which includes the following additional (optional) items:

The Lesson

There are several readings from the Holy Bible, being generally considered as appropriate for inclusion in a Marriage Service; however, probably the most popular and appropriate is St. Paul's definition of love. Although it is from The New Testament, you will even find that, where one of the parties to be married is Jewish, there will invariably be no objections to your choosing this one for their Service as well.

It is to be found in various translations; however, personally, I prefer to use the following which is in clear and natural present-day English:

"Love is patient; love is kind and envies no one. Love is never boastful, nor conceited, nor rude; never selfish, not quick to take offence. Love keeps no score of wrongs; does not gloat over other men's sins, but delights in the truth. There is nothing love cannot face; there is no limit to its faith, its hope, and its endurance. Love will never come to an end.

There are three things that last for ever: faith, hope, and love; but the greatest of them all is love." "Thanks be to God."

The Rings - Explanation

It can be most beneficial, not only for the couple being married, but also for the enlightenment of many of their family and friends in attendance, to hear something more concerning the significance of the Wedding Ring(s) in the marriage. Probably the best (simple) explanation I have ever heard is that which was included in an original service composed by Dr. A.T. DeGroot Distinguished Professor of Church History, Brite Divinity School, at Texas Christian University. Ideally, it is best used when there are to be two rings rather than only the one Wedding Ring.

Firstly, while holding the Wedding Ring, before handing it to the 'groom to place on the bride's finger, the Chaplain shall say:

"In the providence of God, and for the fullest happiness of the home, there are ways in which the husband is the head of the wife. He imparts unto her his name, and receives her into his care and protection - in token of which he gives her this ring in pledge.

Thus are you, _____ [Bridegroom], to compass about her life with strength and protecting love. Thus are you, _____ [Bride], to wear this ring as the enclosing bond of reverence and dearest faith - both fulfilling the perfect circle of duty that makes you one."

Later, while holding the Second (Wedding) Ring, before handing it to the bride to place on the bridegroom's finger, the Minister shall say:

"Because the man becomes to the woman her companion in all of life's experience, and is henceforth distinguished by his devotion to her, he wears this ring *as the mark of his faithfulness.*"

A Scottish Poem

Several years ago, I came across this poem [Anon.] in a Scottish Newspaper and, shortly having a marriage to perform between a bridegroom from London [England] and a bride from Edinburgh [Scotland], it seemed most appropriate to insert it immediately before the Benediction.   You are most unlikely to find this used in any Marriage Service other than in one of mine, or in one performed by any my colleagues who have chosen to adopt its use in theirs.

It reads as follows:

"Now you will feel no rain, for each of you will be shelter for the other; Now you will feel no cold, for each of you will be warmth for the other; Now there will be no more loneliness, for though you are two persons, there is only one life before you.   Go now to your dwelling place and enter into the days of your life together."

I have since heard this poem claimed to be "An Apache Prayer" - albeit with slightly different wording.   However, whether the Scots brought it with them to North America and the Apache adopted it, or some Scot who came over here, got it from the Apache and 'took it home' with him - who can say ?

I have also found this a quite delightful 'rounding off' to any marriage service wherein, for one reason or another [e.g. a Civil Wedding], the Benediction is not being given to end the service.

Blessing of the Wedding Ring(s)

Both the shortest version and the slightly longer version of the service as reproduced in this chapter, are set down allowing for two rings being used.

If there is only *one ring* to be given [i.e. from Bridegroom to Bride] then as soon as the 'groom has given it, the minister *may* then add a blessing as follows:

"Bless, O Lord, this Ring, that he who gives it and she who wears it may abide in thy peace, and continue in thy favour, unto their life's end;   through Jesus Christ our Lord.   Amen."

If there are *two rings* to be given [i.e. to include one also from bride to bridegroom] then after both rings have been give, the minister *may* then add a blessing as follows:

"Bless, O Lord, these Rings, that they who wear them may abide in thy peace, and continue in thy favour, unto their life's end: through Jesus Christ our Lord.   Amen."

In both cases [one ring or two] the services set down [exampled] in this book provide for the Blessing of the Ring(s) *after* the rings have been exchanged - and in these instances, the minister would have the couple join their 'ring hands' together and place his right hand over them, to say the Blessing.   He may also, if wearing the Stole [A Vestment consisting of a long strip with ends hanging down from back of the neck - usually with a Cross at each end], wrap the ends around their hands whilst blessing the rings.

Alternatively, if only the one Wedding Ring is to be used, the minister may instead, upon receiving the ring from the 'Best Man' (or Ring Bearer) first place it upon 'the book' [Prayer Book, or Book of the Service] he is holding, and perform the aforementioned Blessing of the Ring, *before* handing it to the 'groom to place on the bride's finger.

Christian (or Given) Names

In all of the Christian (and most other Religious) Services for marriage, whether taking place in a church or not, one *does not use* an individual's Surname [Last Name] but only his/her 'Christian' (or 'Given') Names - the names by which they are known to God.   Neither does one use 'nicknames' or any common abbreviations of their proper names.

Thus, they are not to say "I, John Henry Jones, take thee Mary Ann Smith.." but simply "I, John Henry, take thee Mary Ann...etc."

You will occasionally be asked, by someone who 'absolutely hates' one of his/her names, that you leave it out.   Well, there are hundreds of fellows called "John" but not so many called "John Henry", so you should endeavour to persuade the individual who is 'complaining' that, for this special occasion "before God", it is only fitting that he/she makes his/her vows using all of his/her given names, in full and unadulterated.

On the other hand, for a Civil Marriage, you should include use of their Surnames [Last Names] since in this case, the couple are entering into a contract recognized only by Civil Law.

Blessing of a Civil Marriage ?

There are of course services to be found and referred to as the "Order for Blessing of a Civil Marriage."   That is to say, for use sometime after the event - as distinct from calling upon God for his blessing of the union at the end of an (otherwise) non-religious service.

Whenever a couple come to me, having sometime previously been legally married *other than* in a Religious Service *and* by a Minister of Religion, I always take the view with them that - whilst they are indeed married "in the eyes of the State" [i.e. by Civil Law] they have *not yet been married* "before God."   In short, being "not married", I can perform a marriage for them *as if* they were in all respects still 'single'.

The only difference between my performing a marriage for them and, my performing a marriage for any other still (legally) single persons is in the matter of the Marriage Licence.   Since they are already 'married' under the law, they do not need a licence for me to marry them now.

Nevertheless, in order that I shall not find I have, albeit unknowingly and in good faith, performed a marriage between a couple who *are not* already legally married and without a licence, I must insist upon first having in my possession [for my retention on file] a "Certified Copy" of their original "Licence and Certificate of Marriage", (not simply an ordinary "Marriage Certificate") to *confirm* that they are in fact already married.

"And be Loyal Unto Thee"

Finally in this chapter, there is set down the same 'Traditional' Service, but in a *'modified version'* substituting the words "and be loyal unto thee" instead of "and to obey" in the woman's vows.

Reaffirmation of Marriage Vows

This is an entirely different matter, and is dealt with in Chapter Twelve of this book.

THE MARRIAGE SERVICE
[SOLEMNIZATION OF HOLY MATRIMONY]
THE ORDER FOR MARRIAGE
[TRADITIONAL]
[SIMPLIFIED SERVICE FOR BOTH ANGLICAN AND CATHOLIC]

47

¶ *At the proper time and place appointed, the man and the woman to be married, having been qualified according to the laws of the State and the standards of the Church, shall stand facing the Chaplain [Minister], the man at the Chaplain's left hand and the woman at his right hand.*

THE MARRIAGE SERVICE

¶ *The Chaplain shall say:*

In the Name of the Father, and of the Son, and of the Holy Ghost. Amen.

¶ *Then addressing the company, he shall say:*

Dearly beloved, we are gathered together here in the sight of God, and in the face of this company, to join together this man and this woman in holy Matrimony, which is an honourable estate, instituted of God, signifying unto us the mystical union that is betwixt Christ and his Church, which holy estate Christ adorned and beautified with his presence and first miracle that he wrought in Cana of Galilee, and is commended of St. Paul to be honourable among all men: and therefore is not by any to be entered into unadvisedly or lightly; but reverently, discreetly, advisedly, soberly, and in the fear of God. Into this holy estate these two persons present come now to be joined. If any man can show just cause, why they may not lawfully be joined together, let him now speak, or else hereafter forever hold his peace.

¶ *Then, addressing the persons to be married, he shall say:*

I require and charge you both, as ye will answer at the dreadful day of judgement when the secrets of all hearts shall be disclosed, that if either of you know any impediment, why ye may not be lawfully joined together in Matrimony, ye do now confess it. For be ye well assured, that if any persons are joined together otherwise than as God's Word doth allow, their marriage is not lawful.

¶ *If no sufficient impediment be alleged, the Chaplain shall say unto the man:*

_____, Wilt thou have this woman to thy wedded wife, to live together after God's ordinance in the holy estate of Matrimony? Wilt thou love her, comfort her, honour, and keep her, in sickness and in health; and, forsaking all others, keep thee only unto her, so long as ye both shall live ?

¶ *Then the man shall answer:*

I will.

¶ Then the Chaplain shall say unto the woman:

_____, Wilt thou have this man to thy wedded husband, to live together after God's ordinance in the holy estate of Matrimony ?   Wilt thou obey him, and serve him, love, honour, and keep him, in sickness and in health; and, forsaking all others, keep thee only unto him, so long as ye both shall live ?

¶ The woman shall answer:

I will.

¶ Then the Chaplain shall say:

Who giveth this woman to be married to this man ?

¶ Then the Bride's father (or friend) presenting her shall answer:

I do.   [Alt: "Her mother and I do."]

¶ Then the Chaplain, receiving the woman at her father's (or friend's) hand, shall cause the man with his right hand to take the woman by her right hand, and to say after him as follows:

I, _____, take thee, _____, to my wedded Wife, to have and to hold from this day forward, for better for worse, for richer for poorer, in sickness and in health, to love, and to cherish, 'till death us do part, according to God's holy ordinance; and thereto I plight thee my troth.

¶ Then shall they loose their hands; and the woman with her right hand taking the man by his right hand, shall say after the Chaplain:

I, _____, take thee, _____, to my wedded Husband, to have and to hold from this day forward, for better for worse, for richer for poorer, in sickness and in health, to love, cherish and to obey, 'till death us do part, according to God's holy ordinance; and thereto I give thee my troth.

*¶ The Chaplain will now secure the Wedding Ring from the Best Man [or the Ring Bearer] and hand it to the man, who places it on the woman's fourth finger of her left hand and, **holding it there**, shall say after the Chaplain:*

With this ring I thee wed; with my body I thee worship; and with all my worldly goods I thee endow: In the name of the Father, and of the Son, and of the Holy Ghost.   Amen.

*¶ The Chaplain will now secure the Second Ring from the Maid (Matron) of Honour [or the Ring Bearer] and hand it to the woman, who places it on the fourth finger of the man's left hand and, **holding it there**, shall say after the Chaplain:*

With this ring I thee wed: In the name of the Father, and of the Son, and of the Holy Ghost.   Amen.

¶ Then the Chaplain may say:

Bless, O Lord, these Rings, that they who wear them may abide in thy peace, and continue in thy favour, unto their life's end: through Jesus Christ our Lord. Amen.

¶ Then the Chaplain shall say:

Let us Pray.

Then shall the Chaplain and the people, still standing, say the Lord's Prayer.

Our Father, which art in heaven, Hallowed be thy Name. Thy kingdom come. Thy will be done, On earth as it is in heaven. Give us this day our daily bread. And forgive us our trespasses, As we forgive them that trespass against us. And lead us not into temptation, But deliver us from evil. For thine is the kingdom, and the power, and the glory, for ever and ever. Amen.

¶ Then shall the Chaplain add,

O Eternal God, Creator and Preserver of all mankind, Giver of all spiritual grace, the Author of everlasting life; Send thy blessing upon these thy servants, this man and this woman, whom we bless in thy Name, that they, living faithfully together, may surely perform and keep the vow and covenant betwixt them made, and may ever remain in perfect love and peace together, and live according to thy laws; through Jesus Christ our Lord. Amen.

¶ Then shall the Chaplain join their right hands together and say,

Those whom God hath joined together let no man put asunder,

¶ Then shall the Chaplain speak unto the company,

Forasmuch as _____ and _____ have consented together in holy wedlock, and have witnessed the same before God and this company, and thereto have given and pledged their troth, each to the other, and have declared the same by giving a receiving a Ring, and by joining hands; I pronounce that they are Man and Wife, in the Name of the Father, and of the Son, and of the Holy Ghost. Amen.

¶ Then the Man and the Wife kneeling, the Chaplain shall add this Blessing,

God the Father, God the Son, God the Holy Ghost, bless, preserve, and keep you; the Lord mercifully with his favour look upon you, and so fill you with all spiritual benediction and grace, that ye may so live together in this life, that in the world to come ye may have life everlasting. AMEN.

PRESENTATION

Ladies and Gentlemen, I now have the honour to present to you:

MR. AND MRS. _____.

¶   *At the proper time and place appointed, the man and the woman to be married, having been qualified according to the laws of the State and the standards of the Church, shall stand facing the Chaplain [Minister], the man at the Chaplain's left hand and the woman at his right hand.*

THE MARRIAGE SERVICE

¶   *The Chaplain shall say:*

In the Name of the Father, and of the Son, and of the Holy Ghost. Amen.

¶   *Then addressing the company, he shall say:*

Dearly beloved, we are gathered together here in the sight of God, and in the face of this company, to join together this man and this woman in holy Matrimony, which is an honourable estate, instituted of God, signifying unto us the mystical union that is betwixt Christ and his Church, which holy estate Christ adorned and beautified with his presence and first miracle that he wrought in Cana of Galilee, and is commended of St. Paul to be honourable among all men: and therefore is not by any to be entered into unadvisedly or lightly;   but reverently, discreetly, advisedly, soberly, and in the fear of God.   Into this holy estate these two persons present come now to be joined.   If any man can show just cause, why they may not lawfully be joined together, let him now speak, or else hereafter forever hold his peace.

¶   *Then, addressing the persons to be married, he shall say:*

I require and charge you both, as ye will answer at the dreadful day of judgement when the secrets of all hearts shall be disclosed, that if either of you know any impediment, why ye may not be lawfully joined together in Matrimony, ye do now confess it.   For be ye well assured, that if any persons are joined together otherwise than as God's Word doth allow, their marriage is not lawful.

¶   *If no sufficient impediment be alleged, the Chaplain shall say unto the man:*

_____, Wilt thou have this woman to thy wedded wife, to live together after God's ordinance in the holy estate of Matrimony ?   Wilt thou love her, comfort her, honour, and keep her, in sickness and in health;   and, forsaking all others, keep thee only unto her, so long as ye both shall live ?

¶   *Then the man shall answer:*

I will.

¶ *Then the Chaplain shall say unto the woman:*

_____, Wilt thou have this man to thy wedded husband, to live together after God's ordinance in the holy estate of Matrimony ? Wilt thou obey him, and serve him, love, honour, and keep him, in sickness and in health; and, forsaking all others, keep thee only unto him, so long as ye both shall live ?

¶ *The woman shall answer:*

I will.

¶ *Then the Chaplain shall say:*

Who giveth this woman to be married to this man ?

¶ *Then the Bride's father (or friend) presenting her shall answer:*

I do. [Alt: "Her mother and I do."]

¶ *Then the Chaplain, receiving the woman at her father's (or friend's) hand, shall cause the man with his right hand to take the woman by her right hand, and to say after him as follows:*

I, _____, take thee, _____, to my wedded Wife, to have and to hold from this day forward, for better for worse, for richer for poorer, in sickness and in health, to love, and to cherish, 'till death us do part, according to God's holy ordinance; and thereto I plight thee my troth.

¶ *Then shall they loose their hands; and the woman with her right hand taking the man by his right hand, shall say after the Chaplain:*

I, _____, take thee, _____, to my wedded Husband, to have and to hold from this day forward, for better for worse, for richer for poorer, in sickness and in health, to love, cherish and to obey, 'till death us do part, according to God's holy ordinance; and thereto I give thee my troth.

¶ *The Chaplain will now secure the Wedding Ring from the Best Man [or the Ring Bearer] and, retaining it for the moment, addresses the company at large, and the Bride and 'Groom in particular, as follows:-*

In the providence of God, and for the fullest happiness of the home, there are ways in which the Husband is the Head of the Wife. He imparts unto her his name, and receives her into his care and protection — in token of which he gives her this ring in pledge.

Thus are you, _____ [Bridegroom], to compass about her life with strength and protecting love. Thus are you, _____ [Bride], to wear this ring as the enclosing bond of reverence and dearest faith — both fulfilling the perfect circle of duty that makes you one.

¶ *The Chaplain now hands the ring to the man who places it on the woman's fourth finger of her left hand and, **holding it there**, shall say after the Chaplain:*

With this ring I thee wed;   with my body I thee worship;   and with all
my worldly goods I thee endow: In the name of the Father, and of the Son,
and of the Holy Ghost.   Amen.

¶   *The Chaplain will now secure the Second Ring from the Maid (Matron) of
Honour [or the Ring Bearer] and, retaining it for a moment, continues to
address the couple as follows:*

Because the man becomes to the woman her companion in all of life's
experience, and is henceforth distinguished by his devotion to her, he
wears this ring as the mark of his faithfulness.

¶   *The Chaplain now hands the Ring to the woman who places it on the fourth
finger of the man's left hand and, **holding it there**, shall say after the
Chaplain:*

With this ring I thee wed: In the name of the Father, and of the Son,
and of the Holy Ghost.   Amen.

¶   *Then the Chaplain may say:*

Bless, O Lord, these Rings, that they who wear them may abide in thy
peace, and continue in thy favour, unto their life's end: through Jesus
Christ our Lord.   Amen.

¶   *Then the Chaplain shall say:*

The Lesson is taken from the First Letter of Paul to the Corinthians,
Chapter 13, Verses 4-8 and 13.

Love is patient;   love is kind and envies no one.   Love is never
boastful, nor conceited, nor rude;   never selfish, not quick to take
offence.   Love keeps no score of wrongs;   does not gloat over other men's
sins, but delights in the truth.   There is nothing love cannot face;
there is no limit to its faith, its hope, and its endurance.   Love will
never come to an end.

There are three things that last for ever: faith, hope, and love;
but the greatest of them all is love.   Thanks [Praise] be to God.

¶   *Then the Chaplain shall say:*

Let us Pray.

*Then shall the Chaplain **and the people**, still standing, **say the Lord's
Prayer**.*

Our Father, which art in heaven, Hallowed be thy Name.   Thy kingdom
come.   Thy will be done, On earth as it is in heaven.   Give us this day
our daily bread.   And forgive us our trespasses, As we forgive them that
trespass against us.   And lead us not into temptation, But deliver us from
evil.   For thine is the kingdom, and the power, and the glory, for ever
and ever.   Amen.

¶   *Then shall the Chaplain add,*

O Eternal God, Creator and Preserver of all mankind, Giver of all spiritual grace, the Author of everlasting life; Send thy blessing upon these thy servants, this man and this woman, whom we bless in thy Name, that they, living faithfully together, may surely perform and keep the vow and covenant betwixt them made, and may ever remain in perfect love and peace together, and live according to thy laws; through Jesus Christ our Lord. Amen.

¶ *Then shall the Chaplain join their right hands together and say,*

Those whom God hath joined together let no man put asunder,

¶ *Then shall the Chaplain speak unto the company,*

Forasmuch as _____ and _____ have consented together in holy wedlock, and have witnessed the same before God and this company, and thereto have given and pledged their troth, each to the other, and have declared the same by giving a receiving a Ring, and by joining hands; I pronounce that they are Man and Wife, in the Name of the Father, and of the Son, and of the Holy Ghost. Amen.

¶ *The Man and the Wife still standing, the Chaplain may say:*

Now you will feel no rain, for each of you will be shelter for the other; Now you will feel no cold, for each of you will be warmth for the other; Now there will be no more loneliness, for though you are two persons, there is only one life before you. Go now to your dwelling place and enter into the days of your life together.

¶ *Then the Man and the Wife kneeling, the Chaplain shall add this Blessing,*

God the Father, God the Son, God the Holy Ghost, bless, preserve, and keep you; the Lord mercifully with his favour look upon you, and so fill you with all spiritual benediction and grace, that ye may so live together in this life, that in the world to come ye may have life everlasting. AMEN.

PRESENTATION

Ladies and Gentlemen, I now have the honour to present to you:

MR. AND MRS. _____.
_____T. 2

THE MARRIAGE SERVICE
[SOLEMNIZATION OF HOLY MATRIMONY]
THE ORDER FOR MARRIAGE
[MODIFIED TRADITIONAL — WITH ADDITIONS]
[SIMPLIFIED SERVICE FOR BOTH ANGLICAN AND CATHOLIC]

55

¶ *At the proper time and place appointed, the man and the woman to be married, having been qualified according to the laws of the State and the standards of the Church, shall stand **facing the Chaplain** [Minister], the man at the Chaplain's left hand and the woman at his right hand.*

THE MARRIAGE SERVICE

¶ *The Chaplain shall say:*

In the Name of the Father, and of the Son, and of the Holy Ghost. Amen.

¶ *Then addressing the company, he shall say:*

Dearly beloved, we are gathered together here in the sight of God, and in the face of this company, to join together this man and this woman in holy Matrimony, which is an honourable estate, instituted of God, signifying unto us the mystical union that is betwixt Christ and his Church, which holy estate Christ adorned and beautified with his presence and first miracle that he wrought in Cana of Galilee, and is commended of St. Paul to be honourable among all men: and therefore is not by any to be entered into unadvisedly or lightly; but reverently, discreetly, advisedly, soberly, and in the fear of God. Into this holy estate these two persons present come now to be joined. If any man can show just cause, why they may not lawfully be joined together, let him now speak, or else hereafter forever hold his peace.

¶ *Then, addressing the persons to be married, he shall say:*

I require and charge you both, as ye will answer at the dreadful day of judgement when the secrets of all hearts shall be disclosed, that if either of you know any impediment, why ye may not be lawfully joined together in Matrimony, ye do now confess it. For be ye well assured, that if any persons are joined together otherwise than as God's Word doth allow, their marriage is not lawful.

¶ *If no sufficient impediment be alleged, the Chaplain shall say unto the man:*

_____, Wilt thou have this woman to thy wedded wife, to live together after God's ordinance in the holy estate of Matrimony ? Wilt thou love her, comfort her, honour, and keep her, in sickness and in health; and, forsaking all others, keep thee only unto her, so long as ye both shall live ?

¶ *Then the man shall answer:*

I will.

¶ *Then the Chaplain shall say unto the woman:*

_____, Wilt thou have this man to thy wedded husband, to live together after God's ordinance in the holy estate of Matrimony ? Wilt thou be loyal unto him, love, honour, and keep him, in sickness and in health; and, forsaking all others, keep thee only unto him, so long as ye both shall live ?

¶ *The woman shall answer:*

I will.

¶ *Then the Chaplain shall say:*

Who giveth this woman to be married to this man ?

¶ *Then the Bride's father (or friend) presenting her shall answer:*

I do. [Alt: "Her mother and I do."]

¶ *Then the Chaplain, receiving the woman at her father's (or friend's) hand, shall cause the man with his right hand to take the woman by her right hand, and to say after him as follows:*

I, _____, take thee, _____, to my wedded Wife, to have and to hold from this day forward, for better for worse, for richer for poorer, in sickness and in health, to love, and to cherish, 'till death us do part, according to God's holy ordinance; and thereto I plight thee my troth.

¶ *Then shall they loose their hands; and the woman with her right hand taking the man by his right hand, shall say after the Chaplain:*

I, _____, take thee, _____, to my wedded Husband, to have and to hold from this day forward, for better for worse, for richer for poorer, in sickness and in health, to love, cherish and be loyal unto thee, 'till death us do part, according to God's holy ordinance; and thereto I give thee my troth.

¶ *The Chaplain will now secure the Wedding Ring from the Best Man [or the Ring Bearer] and, retaining it for the moment, addresses the company at large, and the Bride and 'Groom in particular, as follows:-*

In the providence of God, and for the fullest happiness of the home, there are ways in which the Husband is the Head of the Wife. He imparts unto her his name, and receives her into his care and protection - in token of which he gives her this ring in pledge.

Thus are you, _____ [Bridegroom], to compass about her life with strength and protecting love. Thus are you, _____ [Bride], to wear this ring as the enclosing bond of reverence and dearest faith - both fulfilling the perfect circle of duty that makes you one.

¶ *The Chaplain now hands the ring to the man who places it on the woman's fourth finger of her left hand and, **holding it there**, shall say after the Chaplain:*

With this ring I thee wed; with my body I thee worship; and with all my worldly goods I thee endow: In the name of the Father, and of the Son, and of the Holy Ghost. Amen.

¶ *The Chaplain will now secure the Second Ring from the Maid (Matron) of Honour [or the Ring Bearer] and, retaining it for a moment, continues to address the couple as follows:*

Because the man becomes to the woman her companion in all of life's experience, and is henceforth distinguished by his devotion to her, he wears this ring as the mark of his faithfulness.

¶ *The Chaplain now hands the Ring to the woman who places it on the fourth finger of the man's left hand and,* **holding it there,** *shall say after the Chaplain:*

With this ring I thee wed: In the name of the Father, and of the Son, and of the Holy Ghost. Amen.

¶ *Then the Chaplain may say:*

Bless, O Lord, these Rings, that they who wear them may abide in thy peace, and continue in thy favour, unto their life's end: through Jesus Christ our Lord. Amen.

¶ *Then the Chaplain shall say:*

The Lesson is taken from the First Letter of Paul to the Corinthians, Chapter 13, Verses 4-8 and 13.

Love is patient; love is kind and envies no one. Love is never boastful, nor conceited, nor rude; never selfish, not quick to take offence. Love keeps no score of wrongs; does not gloat over other men's sins, but delights in the truth. There is nothing love cannot face; there is no limit to its faith, its hope, and its endurance. Love will never come to an end.

There are three things that last for ever: faith, hope, and love; but the greatest of them all is love. Thanks [Praise] be to God.

¶ *Then the Chaplain shall say:*

Let us Pray.

Then shall the Chaplain **and the people,** *still standing,* **say the Lord's Prayer.**

Our Father, which art in heaven, Hallowed be thy Name. Thy kingdom come. Thy will be done, On earth as it is in heaven. Give us this day our daily bread. And forgive us our trespasses, As we forgive them that trespass against us. And lead us not into temptation, But deliver us from evil. For thine is the kingdom, and the power, and the glory, for ever and ever. Amen.

¶ *Then shall the Chaplain add,*

O Eternal God, Creator and Preserver of all mankind, Giver of all spiritual grace, the Author of everlasting life; Send thy blessing upon these thy servants, this man and this woman, whom we bless in thy Name, that they, living faithfully together, may surely perform and keep the vow and covenant betwixt them made, and may ever remain in perfect love and peace together, and live according to thy laws; through Jesus Christ our Lord. Amen.

¶ *Then shall the Chaplain join their right hands together and say,*

Those whom God hath joined together let no man put asunder,

¶ *Then shall the Chaplain speak unto the company,*

Forasmuch as _____ and _____ have consented together in holy wedlock, and have witnessed the same before God and this company, and thereto have given and pledged their troth, each to the other, and have declared the same by giving a receiving a Ring, and by joining hands; I pronounce that they are Man and Wife, in the Name of the Father, and of the Son, and of the Holy Ghost. Amen.

¶ *The Man and the Wife still standing, the Chaplain may say:*

Now you will feel no rain, for each of you will be shelter for the other; Now you will feel no cold, for each of you will be warmth for the other; Now there will be no more loneliness, for though you are two persons, there is only one life before you. Go now to your dwelling place and enter into the days of your life together.

¶ *Then the Man and the Wife kneeling, the Chaplain shall add this Blessing,*

God the Father, God the Son, God the Holy Ghost, bless, preserve, and keep you; the Lord mercifully with his favour look upon you, and so fill you with all spiritual benediction and grace, that ye may so live together in this life, that in the world to come ye may have life everlasting. AMEN.

PRESENTATION

Ladies and Gentlemen, I now have the honour to present to you:

MR. AND MRS. _____.

THE 'TRADITIONAL' ORDER OF SERVICE
[MODERN VERSION]

The 'Modern Version' of the otherwise 'Traditional' Marriage Service is, of course, for those who *do not* wish to have the original version which includes the "obey" in the woman's vows - this also requires that the further undertaking from the man in the Ring Ceremony must be deleted.

In recent years, this has been the more "popular" version in recognition of the "equality of the sexes" - despite the risks involved (as explained in Chapters Three and Four) by omission of those very special pledges.

Of course it remains the more popular, and will obviously continue to be so where the couple's chosen minister may not take the time to go into detail with them at interview beforehand, as to precisely what is really meant by those very special pledges.   It's quite remarkable how many young people have it in their minds that the original version has now somehow been "phased out."   *Political and sociological measures* cannot "phase out" *God's* teaching !

However, I have found that the pendulum is at last fast swinging back in many quarters, with couples [young and old alike] wishing to return to "the good old standards" of truth and morality in the home - all the moreso by reason of these being seemingly so lacking in present-day society as an whole.

More are now taking their time in finding the right partner "for life" before getting married (or married again, as the case may be) - instead of rushing into it, with the proviso [in the back of their minds] that, if it doesn't work out, they can get divorced and try again with someone else.

Having performed literally hundreds of marriages;   details of all of which are recorded in my computer, I have been able to follow the changing trends in couples' requirements.   It may interest some ministers to know that, whereas as recently as 1987, 54% of all the marriages I performed in that year chose to have the 'original version' [i.e. including the 'obey' etc.] - by 1990, this percentage had increased to 86% and, in 1991, it had risen to no less than 95% !

This is taking into account also the many non-denominational [substitute 'Inter Faith' services] between Christians and those of other faiths [e.g. Jewish, Buddhist, etc.] where they also requested that I include those same special pledges to each other.

Nevertheless, there'll always be those who want to have the 'modern version' and after all, it's their Wedding, not yours !   Having done your duty as a minister to explain the differences - don't press the matter further.   It must be of their own free will [i.e. of *both* parties] that they choose either the 'original' or the 'modern' version - or of any other type of service, for that matter - for their own Wedding.

Here follows two such 'modern' versions of the old Traditional Christian Service - firstly a short or 'basic' service, followed by another in which is included the Lesson and, the 'Scottish' Poem.   However, in the latter, the additional narrative concerning the rings has been omitted - since this would also add a connotation of the 'obey'.

In the second version however, in the Ring Ceremony from the man, there is included a 'modified' (version of the traditional) undertaking from the man, as follows:

‡   "With this ring I thee wed; with my body I thee honour;   and, all my worldly goods with thee I share: In the name of the Father, and of the Son, and of the Holy Ghost.   Amen."

This being where the "obey" is *not included* in the woman's vows, but where the man nevertheless wishes to make such an undertaking to his bride.   The difference is subtle inasmuch as, it reads "with my body I thee *honour*" instead of "with my body I thee *worship*"; and "all my worldly goods with thee I *share*", instead of " with all my worldly goods I thee *endow.*"

Thus, *not quite* such an all-embracing undertaking as is given in the original version — having a subtle, but nevertheless significant difference in its meaning.

Incidentally, some couples do need to have it explained to them that the word "Worship" *does not* mean "Pray".   It means "Serve."   In 'worshipping' God, as also when we 'pray' to Him, we are 'serving' God.   Thus, when the 'groom says "with my body I thee worship", he is undertaking to 'serve' his wife, by doing all that he can physically to take care of her.

‡ FOOTNOTE:

THIS WAS THE VERSION USED FOR H.R.H. THE PRINCE CHARLES IN HIS MARRIAGE TO LADY DIANA SPENCER - IN ST. PAUL'S CATHEDRAL ON 29TH JULY, 1981.   IN SHORT, HE *DID NOT* 'ENDOW HER' WITH 'ALL HIS WORLDLY GOODS'.   IN HIS PARTICULAR CASE, MUCH OF WHAT IS PRESENTLY HIS, IS ONLY HIS THROUGH HIS LIFETIME - AND CANNOT BE 'ENDOWED' TO HIS WIFE.

[SOLEMNIZATION OF HOLY MATRIMONY]
THE ORDER FOR MARRIAGE
[TRADITIONAL — MODERN VERSION]
[SIMPLIFIED SERVICE FOR BOTH ANGLICAN AND CATHOLIC]

¶ *At the proper time and place appointed, the man and the woman to be married, having been qualified according to the laws of the State and the standards of the Church, shall stand facing the Minister [Chaplain], the man at the Chaplain's left hand and the woman at his right hand.*

THE MARRIAGE SERVICE

¶ *The Chaplain shall say:*

In the Name of the Father, and of the Son, and of the Holy Ghost. Amen.

¶ *Then addressing the company, he shall say:*

Dearly beloved, we are gathered together here in the sight of God, and in the face of this company, to join together this man and this woman in holy Matrimony, which is an honourable estate, instituted of God, signifying unto us the mystical union that is betwixt Christ and his Church, which holy estate Christ adorned and beautified with his presence and first miracle that he wrought in Cana of Galilee, and is commended of St. Paul to be honourable among all men: and therefore is not by any to be entered into unadvisedly or lightly; but reverently, discreetly, advisedly, soberly, and in the fear of God. Into this holy estate these two persons present come now to be joined. If any man can show just cause, why they may not lawfully be joined together, let him now speak, or else hereafter forever hold his peace.

¶ *Then, addressing the persons to be married, he shall say:*

I require and charge you both, as ye will answer at the dreadful day of judgement when the secrets of all hearts shall be disclosed, that if either of you know any impediment, why ye may not be lawfully joined together in Matrimony, ye do now confess it. For be ye well assured, that if any persons are joined together otherwise than as God's Word doth allow, their marriage is not lawful.

¶ *If no sufficient impediment be alleged, the Chaplain shall say unto the man:*

_____, Wilt thou have this woman to thy wedded wife, to live together after God's ordinance in the holy estate of Matrimony ? Wilt thou love her, comfort her, honour, and keep her, in sickness and in health; and, forsaking all others, keep thee only unto her, so long as ye both shall live ?

¶ *Then the man shall answer:*

I will.

¶   *Then the Chaplain shall say unto the woman:*

_____, Wilt thou have this man to thy wedded husband, to live together after God's ordinance in the holy estate of Matrimony ?   Wilt thou love him, comfort him, honour, and keep him, in sickness and in health;   and, forsaking all others, keep thee only unto him, so long as ye both shall live ?

¶   *The woman shall answer:*

   I will.

¶   *Then the Chaplain shall say:*

   Who giveth this woman to be married to this man ?

¶   *Then the Bride's father (or friend) presenting her shall answer:*

   I do.   [Alt: "Her mother and I do."]

¶   *Then the Chaplain, receiving the woman at her father's (or friend's) hand, shall cause the man with his right hand to take the woman by her right hand, and to say after him as follows:*

   I, _____, take thee, _____, to my wedded Wife, to have and to hold from this day forward, for better for worse, for richer for poorer, in sickness and in health, to love, and to cherish, 'till death us do part, according to God's holy ordinance;   and thereto I plight thee my troth.

¶   *Then shall they loose their hands;   and the woman with her right hand taking the man by his right hand, shall say after the Chaplain:*

   I, _____, take thee, _____, to my wedded Husband, to have and to hold from this day forward, for better for worse, for richer for poorer, in sickness and in health, to love, and to cherish, 'till death us do part, according to God's holy ordinance;   and thereto I give thee my troth.

¶   *The Chaplain will now secure the Wedding Ring from the Best Man [or the Ring Bearer] and hand it to the man, who places it on the woman's fourth finger of her left hand and,* **holding it there,** *shall say after the Chaplain:*

   With this ring I thee wed;   In the name of the Father, and of the Son, and of the Holy Ghost.   Amen.

¶   *The Chaplain will now secure the Second Ring from the Maid (Matron) of Honour [or the Ring Bearer] and hand it to the woman, who places it on the fourth finger of the man's left hand and,* **holding it there,** *shall say after the Chaplain:*

   With this ring I thee wed: In the name of the Father, and of the Son, and of the Holy Ghost.   Amen.

¶   *Then the Chaplain may say:*

Bless, O Lord, these Rings, that they who wear them may abide in thy peace, and continue in thy favour, unto their life's end: through Jesus Christ our Lord. Amen.

¶ *Then the Chaplain shall say:*

Let us Pray.

Then shall the Chaplain and the people, still standing, say the Lord's Prayer.

Our Father, which art in heaven, Hallowed be thy Name. Thy kingdom come. Thy will be done, On earth as it is in heaven. Give us this day our daily bread. And forgive us our trespasses, As we forgive them that trespass against us. And lead us not into temptation, But deliver us from evil. For thine is the kingdom, and the power, and the glory, for ever and ever. Amen.

¶ *Then shall the Chaplain add,*

O Eternal God, Creator and Preserver of all mankind, Giver of all spiritual grace, the Author of everlasting life; Send thy blessing upon these thy servants, this man and this woman, whom we bless in thy Name, that they, living faithfully together, may surely perform and keep the vow and covenant betwixt them made, and may ever remain in perfect love and peace together, and live according to thy laws; through Jesus Christ our Lord. Amen.

¶ *Then shall the Chaplain join their right hands together and say,*

Those whom God hath joined together let no man put asunder,

¶ *Then shall the Chaplain speak unto the company,*

Forasmuch as _____ and _____ have consented together in holy wedlock, and have witnessed the same before God and this company, and thereto have given and pledged their troth, each to the other, and have declared the same by giving a receiving a Ring, and by joining hands; I pronounce that they are Man and Wife, in the Name of the Father, and of the Son, and of the Holy Ghost. Amen.

¶ *Then the Man and the Wife kneeling, the Chaplain shall add this Blessing,*

God the Father, God the Son, God the Holy Ghost, bless, preserve, and keep you; the Lord mercifully with his favour look upon you, and so fill you with all spiritual benediction and grace, that ye may so live together in this life, that in the world to come ye may have life everlasting. AMEN.

PRESENTATION

Ladies and Gentlemen, I now have the honour to present to you:

MR. AND MRS. _____.

THE MARRIAGE SERVICE
[SOLEMNIZATION OF HOLY MATRIMONY]
THE ORDER FOR MARRIAGE
[TRADITIONAL - MODERN VERSION - WITH ADDITIONS]
[SIMPLIFIED SERVICE FOR BOTH ANGLICAN AND CATHOLIC]

65

¶ *At the proper time and place appointed, the man and the woman to be married, having been qualified according to the laws of the State and the standards of the Church, shall stand* **facing the Minister** *[Chaplain], the man at the Chaplain's left hand and the woman at his right hand.*

THE MARRIAGE SERVICE

¶ *The Chaplain shall say:*

In the Name of the Father, and of the Son, and of the Holy Ghost. Amen.

¶ *Then addressing the company, he shall say:*

Dearly beloved, we are gathered together here in the sight of God, and in the face of this company, to join together this man and this woman in holy Matrimony, which is an honourable estate, instituted of God, signifying unto us the mystical union that is betwixt Christ and his Church, which holy estate Christ adorned and beautified with his presence and first miracle that he wrought in Cana of Galilee, and is commended of St. Paul to be honourable among all men: and therefore is not by any to be entered into unadvisedly or lightly; but reverently, discreetly, advisedly, soberly, and in the fear of God. Into this holy estate these two persons present come now to be joined. If any man can show just cause, why they may not lawfully be joined together, let him now speak, or else hereafter forever hold his peace.

¶ *Then, addressing the persons to be married, he shall say:*

I require and charge you both, as ye will answer at the dreadful day of judgement when the secrets of all hearts shall be disclosed, that if either of you know any impediment, why ye may not be lawfully joined together in Matrimony, ye do now confess it. For be ye well assured, that if any persons are joined together otherwise than as God's Word doth allow, their marriage is not lawful.

¶ *If no sufficient impediment be alleged, the Chaplain shall say unto the* man:

_____, Wilt thou have this woman to thy wedded wife, to live together after God's ordinance in the holy estate of Matrimony ? Wilt thou love her, comfort her, honour, and keep her, in sickness and in health; and, forsaking all others, keep thee only unto her, so long as ye both shall live ?

¶ *Then the man shall answer:*

I will.

¶ *Then the Chaplain shall say unto the woman:*

_____, Wilt thou have this man to thy wedded husband, to live together after God's ordinance in the holy estate of Matrimony ? Wilt thou love him, comfort him, honour, and keep him, in sickness and in health; and, forsaking all others, keep thee only unto him, so long as ye both shall live ?

¶ *The woman shall answer:*

I will.

¶ *Then the Chaplain shall say:*

Who giveth this woman to be married to this man ?

¶ *Then the Bride's father (or friend) presenting her shall answer:*

I do.

¶ *Then the Chaplain, receiving the woman at her father's (or friend's) hand, shall cause the man with his right hand to take the woman by her right hand, and to say after him as follows:*

I, _____, take thee, _____, to my wedded Wife, to have and to hold from this day forward, for better for worse, for richer for poorer, in sickness and in health, to love, and to cherish, 'till death us do part, according to God's holy ordinance; and thereto I plight thee my troth.

¶ *Then shall they loose their hands; and the woman with her right hand taking the man by his right hand, shall say after the Chaplain:*

I, _____, take thee, _____, to my wedded Husband, to have and to hold from this day forward, for better for worse, for richer for poorer, in sickness and in health, to love, and to cherish, 'till death us do part, according to God's holy ordinance; and thereto I give thee my troth.

¶ *The Chaplain will now secure the Wedding Ring from the Best Man [or the Ring Bearer] and hands it to the man who places it on the woman's fourth finger of her left hand and, holding it there, shall say after the Chaplain:*

With this ring I thee wed; with my body I thee honour; and all my worldly goods with thee I share: In the name of the Father, and of the Son, and of the Holy Ghost. Amen.

¶ *The Chaplain will now secure the Second Ring from the Maid (Matron) of Honour [or the Ring Bearer] and hands it to the woman who places it on the fourth finger of the man's left hand and, holding it there, shall say after the Chaplain:*

With this ring I thee wed: In the name of the Father, and of the Son, and of the Holy Ghost. Amen.

¶ Then the Chaplain may say:

Bless, O Lord, these Rings, that they who wear them may abide in thy peace, and continue in thy favour, unto their life's end: through Jesus Christ our Lord. Amen.

¶ Then the Chaplain shall say:

The Lesson is taken from the First Letter of Paul to the Corinthians, Chapter 13, Verses 4-8 and 13.

Love is patient; love is kind and envies no one. Love is never boastful, nor conceited, nor rude; never selfish, not quick to take offence. Love keeps no score of wrongs; does not gloat over other men's sins, but delights in the truth. There is nothing love cannot face; there is no limit to its faith, its hope, and its endurance. Love will never come to an end.

There are three things that last for ever: faith, hope, and love; but the greatest of them all is love. Thanks [Praise] be to God.

¶ Then the Chaplain shall say:

Let us Pray.

*Then shall the Chaplain **and the people**, still standing, **say the Lord's Prayer.***

Our Father, which art in heaven, Hallowed be thy Name. Thy kingdom come. Thy will be done, On earth as it is in heaven. Give us this day our daily bread. And forgive us our trespasses, As we forgive them that trespass against us. And lead us not into temptation, But deliver us from evil. For thine is the kingdom, and the power, and the glory, for ever and ever. Amen.

¶ Then shall the Chaplain add,

O Eternal God, Creator and Preserver of all mankind, Giver of all spiritual grace, the Author of everlasting life; Send thy blessing upon these thy servants, this man and this woman, whom we bless in thy Name, that they, living faithfully together, may surely perform and keep the vow and covenant betwixt them made, and may ever remain in perfect love and peace together, and live according to thy laws; through Jesus Christ our Lord. Amen.

¶ Then shall the Chaplain join their right hands together and say,

Those whom God hath joined together let no man put asunder,

¶ Then shall the Chaplain speak unto the company,

Forasmuch as _____ and _____ have consented together in holy wedlock, and have witnessed the same before God and this company, and thereto have given and pledged their troth, each to the other, and have declared the same by giving a receiving a Ring, and by joining hands; I pronounce that they are Man and Wife, in the Name of the Father, and of the Son, and of the Holy Ghost. Amen.

¶ *The Man and the Wife still standing, the Chaplain may say:*

Now you will feel no rain, for each of you will be shelter for the other; Now you will feel no cold, for each of you will be warmth for the other; Now there will be no more loneliness, for though you are two persons, there is only one life before you. Go now to your dwelling place and enter into the days of your life together.

¶ *Then the Man and the Wife kneeling, the Chaplain shall add this Blessing,*

God the Father, God the Son, God the Holy Ghost, bless, preserve, and keep you; the Lord mercifully with his favour look upon you, and so fill you with all spiritual benediction and grace, that ye may so live together in this life, that in the world to come ye may have life everlasting. AMEN.

PRESENTATION

Ladies and Gentlemen, I now have the honour to present to you:

MR. AND MRS. _____.

——T. 5

A SERVICE FOR CHRISTIAN AND JEW

The form of Special 'Non-Denominational' Service following in this chapter was composed for those who, believing in one and the same God, and wanting a Religious Ceremony, do not want it to include anything that is either specifically Christian or specifically Jewish in reference or context - not least of all not so as to offend any of either their Jewish and/or Christian friends and relations witnessing their marriage.

It contains several parts indicated as optional; also certain words set in parenthesis to indicate them as being optional - according to consensus of the couple and the minister concerned.

This Service can be modified more-or-less 'according to taste' to suit most all 'inter-faith' couples.

It may be interesting to note that, in my own experience of many marriages performed between 'Jew and Gentile' - I can recall *only one* where the Jew required that I delete the Lord's Prayer; and likewise *only one* who had an objection to my including for the Lesson, 1 Corinthians Ch. 13: 4-8, 13 - by reason of it being from the New Testament !   In a few other cases, whilst liking, and wishing to have that particular passage from The New Testament included in the Service - the Jew requested that I simply commence the reading, without the preface announcing from where it was taken !

Incidentally, in almost all of my marriages between Christian and Jew, the Christian has been a Roman Catholic; hardly ever a Protestant, or for that matter, of any other persuasion.   And I'm still trying to determine if there is any particular significance in this, or if purely coincidental.

I'm pleased to be able to say that, this particular 'Order of Service' has been extremely well received by all of the couples for whom I have used it - and by their attendant families and friends.

There are a number of clergy referral services, private yacht charter firms and other establishments who refer couples to me.   Several of them, upon finding that they have before them a couple where one is a Christian and the other is a Jew, and asking if they can recommend someone to officiate in their marriage, promptly reply: "You need our friend Reverend Cunningham."

Then they'll call me to say: "Padre; we have a couple here who need one of your *Jew-Gentile Specials.*"

Incidentally, rather than wearing clerical dress for these occasions, I'll invariably wear Naval uniform instead; even if the marriage is not to take place aboard a ship.

In the ordinary course of events, a regular "Inter-Faith Service" as such, requires the services of both a priest and a rabbi - and takes 'for ever' to conclude.   And if either the bride or the 'groom have been previously married and divorced, they're likely to run into trouble with either the priest and/or the rabbi.   So, the following 'Marriage Service' serves well for such couples - and indeed also for any others who simply do not want to go 'the whole nine yards' encompassing both religions together.

THE MARRIAGE SERVICE 71
[SOLEMNIZATION OF HOLY MATRIMONY]
A SPECIAL 'INTER-FAITH' SERVICE FOR PERSONS WHO,
WHILST BELIEVING IN ONE AND THE SAME GOD,
ONE IS OF THE JEWISH FAITH
AND THE OTHER A CHRISTIAN

¶ *At the proper time and place the man and the woman to be married, having been qualified according to the laws of the State, shall stand **facing the Minister** [Chaplain], the man at the Chaplain's left hand and the woman at his right hand.*

INTRODUCTION

¶ *The Chaplain addressing the company, shall say,*

Friends, we are gathered together here today in the sight of God, within the presence of this company, to join together this man and this woman in Holy Matrimony. It is an honourable Estate, instituted by God, and symbolizing the concern of the whole community of mankind, in the Covenant which they are about to make.

Before we proceed with the actual Service however, I would just like to say that, I am a Chaplain (and Minister of our Lord's Church) and, I am both honoured and most happy to be chosen as the instrument in uniting in marriage two lovely people whose love for each other and whose faith and belief in one and the same God, transcends the fact that one was brought up in the Jewish Faith and, the other a Gentile. **We are all God's children !**

THE MARRIAGE SERVICE

¶ *Then, addressing the persons to be married, he shall say*

This rite of Marriage in which you now come to be united is the first and oldest rite of mankind. Marriage is our foretaste of Paradise, given in the wisdom of God to soothe the troubles and to increase the joys of earthly life. This it will do for you, if you purpose in your hearts to beautify and sweeten it by your tender devotions, your mindfulness in little things, and your patience and sacrifice of self to each other. Coming in full love to the threshold of a new life together, I commend to you these spiritual ministries as the way of lasting happiness.

¶ *Then the Chaplain shall say unto the man,*

Will you, _____, take this woman to be your wedded wife, promising to keep, cherish, and defend her, and to be her faithful and true husband, so long as you both shall live ?

¶ *Then the man shall answer,*

I will.

¶ *Then the Chaplain shall say unto the woman,*

Will you, _____, take this man to be your wedded husband, promising to adhere unalterably to him in all life's changes, *to obey and to serve him [Alt: to be loyal unto him]*, and to be his loving and true wife, so long as you both shall live ?

¶ *The woman shall answer,*

I will.

¶ *Then the Chaplain shall say,*

Who giveth this woman to be married to this man ?

¶ *Then the Chaplain shall receive the woman at the hand of her Father (or friend),* **who shall reply,**

I do. [Alt: "Her Mother and I do."]

¶ *Then the Chaplain shall cause the man to take the woman's right hand in his right hand, and to say after the Chaplain as follows:*

I, _____, take thee _____, to my wedded Wife, to have and to hold from this day forward, for better, for worse, for richer, for poorer, in sickness and in health, to love and to cherish, until death us do part; and thereto I pledge thee my fidelity.

¶ *Then the Chaplain shall cause the woman to take the man's right hand in her right hand, and to say after the Chaplain as follows:*

I, _____, take thee _____, to my wedded Husband, to have and to hold from this day forward, for better, for worse, for richer, for poorer, in sickness and in health, to love, cherish, *and to obey [Alt: and be loyal unto thee]*, until death us do part; and thereto I give thee my fidelity.

¶ *The Chaplain will now secure the Wedding Ring from the Best Man (or the Ring Bearer) and, retaining it for the moment, addresses the company at large, and the Bride and 'Groom in particular, as follows:-*

The Wedding Ring is the outward and visible symbol of your marriage; symbolic of the fact that you have this day pledged yourselves in marriage, signifying to all the uniting of the man and woman in holy matrimony - and, as the ring is a perfect circle without end, it is the fervent prayer of all that your marriage will be as perfect and without end.

In the providence of God, and for the fullest happiness of the home, there are ways in which the husband is the head of the wife. He imparts unto her his name, and receives her into his care and protection - in token of which he gives her this ring in pledge.

Thus are you, _____ [Bridegroom], to compass about her life with strength and protecting love. Thus are you, _____ [Bride], to wear this ring as the enclosing bond of reverence and dearest faith - both fulfilling the perfect circle of duty that makes you one.

¶ *The Chaplain now hands the ring to the man who places it on the woman's fourth finger of her left hand and, holding it there, repeats after the Chaplain: -*

With this Ring I thee wed, with my body I thee worship, and with all my worldly goods I thee endow, as God is my witness.   Amen.

¶ *Then the Chaplain may say,*

Bless, O Lord, this Ring, that he who gives it, and she who wears it, may abide in thy peace, and continue in thy favour, unto their life's end. Amen.

-----------------------------------OPTIONAL----------------------------------

[i.e. If two rings are to be used in the Marriage Service]

¶ *The Chaplain now secures the Second Ring from the Maid (or Matron) of Honour (or the Ring Bearer) and, retaining it for a moment, continues to address the couple as follows:*

Because the man becomes to the woman her companion in all of life's experience, and is henceforth distinguished by his devotion to her, he wears this ring as the mark of his faithfulness.

¶ *The Chaplain now hands the ring to the woman who places it on the fourth finger of the man's left hand and, holding it there, repeats after the Chaplain:*

With this Ring I thee wed, as God is my witness.   Amen.

¶ *Then the Chaplain may say,*

Bless, O Lord, these Rings, that they who wear them may abide in thy peace, and continue in thy favour, unto their life's end.   Amen.

¶ *Then the Chaplain shall say,*

The Lesson is taken from the First Letter of Paul to The Corinthians, Chapter 13, Verses 4 to 8 and 13.

"Love is patient; love is kind and envies no one.   Love is never boastful, nor conceited, nor rude;   never selfish, not quick to take offence.   Love keeps no score of wrongs;   does not gloat over other men's sins, but delights in the truth.   There is nothing love cannot face; there is no limit to its endurance.   Love will never come to an end.

There are three things that last for ever;   faith, hope, and love. But the greatest of them all is love."

Thanks [Praise] be to God.

¶ *Then the Chaplain shall say,*

Let us Pray

*Then shall the Chaplain **and the people,** still standing, **say the Lord's Prayer.***

Our Father, which art in heaven, Hallowed be thy Name. Thy kingdom come. Thy will be done, On earth as it is in heaven. Give us this day our daily bread. And forgive us our trespasses, As we forgive them that trespass against us. And lead us not into temptation, But deliver us from evil. For thine is the kingdom, and the power, and the glory, for ever and ever. Amen.

¶ *Then shall the Chaplain add,*

O Eternal God, Creator and Preserver of all mankind, Giver of all spiritual grace, the Author of everlasting life; Send thy blessing upon these thy servants, this man and this woman, whom we bless in thy Name, that they, living faithfully together, may surely perform and keep the vow and covenant betwixt them made, and may ever remain in perfect love and peace together, and live according to thy laws. Amen.

¶ *Then shall the Chaplain join their right hands together and say,*

Those whom God hath joined together let no man put asunder,

¶ *Then shall the Chaplain speak unto the company,*

Forasmuch as _____ and _____ have now promised to be faithful and true to each other, and have witnessed the same before God and this company, by spoken vows and by giving and receiving a ring in pledge, they are now into a new estate. As a Minister of God's will I now pronounce them to be Husband and Wife.

¶ *Then the Chaplain **may** say unto the Man and his Wife:*

Now you will feel no rain, for each of you will be shelter for the other; Now you will feel no cold, for each of you will be warmth for the other; Now there will be no more loneliness, for 'though you are two persons, there is only one life before you. Go now to your dwelling place and enter into the days of your life together.

¶ *Then the Chaplain shall add this Blessing,*

God Bless, preserve, and keep you; the Lord mercifully with His favour look upon you, and so fill you with all spiritual benediction and grace, that you may so live together in this life, that in the world to come, you may have life everlasting. AMEN.

--------------------------------ALTERNATIVE--------------------------------

¶ *The Chaplain shall now address the Bride/Bridegroom asking her/him:*

_____, are you willing to join your Christian Husband/Wife in receiving the Blessing of The Holy Trinity ?

¶ *Then, if the Bride/'Groom shall reply:*

I am.

¶ *Then the Chaplain shall add this Blessing,*

God the Father, God the Son, God the Holy Ghost, Bless, preserve, and keep you; the Lord mercifully with His favour look upon you, and so fill you with all spiritual benediction and grace, that you may so live together in this life, that in the world to come, you may have life everlasting. AMEN.

------------------------------OPTIONAL------------------------------

The Wine Cup Ceremony

¶ *Then shall the Chaplain receive (from the Bridegroom's supporter or from some other supporter) a glass of red wine, and shall then say unto the Man and his Wife:*

Now may your first act in Holy wedded life be an act of sharing. This cup of wine is symbolic of the cup of life. As you share in this one cup of wine, you agree to share all that the future may bring. All the sweetness life's cup may hold for you should be the sweeter, because you drink it together; whatever drops of bitterness it may contain, should be less bitter because you share them too. As I say the Blessing over the wine, we all pray that God will grant you fullness of joy.

¶ *Then (upon handing the Cup of Wine, first to the Husband), the Minister shall say:*

Almighty God, we praise thee who creates the fruit of the vine a symbol of joy; Bless O Lord this wine and these thy servants who now partake of it in thy Name. Amen.

¶ *Then, when the Wife has drained the glass empty, the Chaplain shall ensure that the glass is first wrapped in a clean white cloth, and shall then hand it back to the Husband to place upon the floor, and break it by stamping upon it.*

PRESENTATION

Chaplain: Ladies and Gentlemen, I now have the honour to present to you:

MR. AND MRS. _____.

---I.I.

NON-DENOMINATIONAL SERVICES

Following in this chapter are two non-denominational services, the first being quite short and informal; the second more formal in structure and comprehensive in content.

In both cases however, as with most Christian Marriage Services, much has been taken from the old 'Traditional' Order of Service, albeit employing more of present-day usage of the English language.

In the second (longer) example, the [optional] affirmation of being "loyal unto thee" is available in the woman's vows, and consequently "with my body I thee worship, and with all my worldly goods I thee endow" also remains available in the ring ceremony from the man.

Include or delete these words as the couple may so prefer - but make quite certain (at interview beforehand) that they fully understand the meaning of these words !

As a Minister of the Gospel, whether non-denominational or otherwise, if you have not already done so, you will undoubtedly develop at least one ceremony that is essentially your own.   Ideally, you need to have at your fingertips, one very short simple one, and another that is more elaborate - in each case to suit the population of the particular area in which you live, and/or for whom you are most often called upon to perform marriages.

When you have found (or developed) the Order of Service with which you are yourself most comfortable, endeavour to use it whenever possible - practice eventually makes for perfection in its delivery, which will help all those present to appreciate this religious service.

Among our many other duties and labours for God, we are in any case in the business of performing marriages *in His name* - commissioned to try and see to it that those participating in the marriages we perform, understand that Christian marriage is in fact Holy Matrimony.   It was not instituted by man, but by God.

Where a marriage is to take place other than in church, it is nevertheless to be performed with due solemnity and decorum.   Having an informal venue for the marriage must not be taken as licence - by anyone - to treat the occasion with any less solemnity than in a church.

Unfortunately, some folks, especially some bride's "modern mothers", if not 'checked', can tend to get somewhat "carried away" in their enthusiasm for organization;   making arrangements with all the supplementary commercial interests involved - to "impress" everyone who'll be attending.

This, to the extent that the 'main event' [i.e. the Marriage Service itself] may be overwhelmed by an irreligious and inappropriate display in such matters as dress, decorations, music, and all manner of other distractions, sometimes even resulting in unseemly conduct by guests and/or any of the actual participants in the service !

When you are asked to use a non-denominational service for a marriage, take care to check that the reason for this is a proper one - and not trivial !

In your 'preamble' to the actual marriage itself, this is where you can, as the officiating minister, best insert your own thoughts and recommendations to a couple — and indeed also for the benefit of present company as an whole.

For example: In the film **"Woman of The Year" (1942)** — Katherine Hepburn, playing a 'leading feminist', was especially moved during the much belated wedding of her parents, upon hearing the 'minister' say:

"You are performing an act of utter faith, believing in one another to the end.

As the bride gives herself to the bridegroom, let him be to her: father and mother, sister and brother, and most sacred husband.

And as he gives himself to her, let the bride inspire and sustain him, let her unite with him in all the experiences of life to which their paths shall lead;   the great moments and the small ones;   that the joys of each shall be the joys of both, and the sorrows of each, the sorrows of both.

If you wish your new estate to be touched with lasting beauty, cherish those gracious visions of your first love;   let them not be blurred by the common events of life.   Be not moved in your devotion;   believe in the ideal;   you saw it once;   it still exists;   it is the final truth."

Consequently, Katherine Hepburn was moved to rush back to her hitherto much neglected husband (Spencer Tracy) with whom she had 'broken up' — having given no serious thought before to either the obligations or the values of marriage.   Now to convince him that, having "heard the words this time" and finally understanding the meaning of marriage, she wanted "to be a real wife" to him.

The fact that these words were used in a movie (and perhaps not taken from any 'real life' event) does not in any way detract from their value.   As I mentioned in my Preface to this book, the opportunities for innovation and to make a service uniquely 'personal' for any particular couple, are almost limitless.

If you sometime read or hear any minister say something during a service or sermon, which you feel is of special value — and which you would like to impart to others yourself — I have yet to meet a minister who would raise any objection to your repeating his words.

If you do use his words, and you can recall his name;   give credit to whom it is due.   If you cannot remember his name, I trust he will forgive you.

Preaching God's word to others is not restricted by any 'copyright' — and similarly, your repeating to others any other words of wisdom you have read or heard, should be far more important than remembering the source !

THE WEDDING CEREMONY
[SOLEMNIZATION OF HOLY MATRIMONY]
THE ORDER FOR MARRIAGE
[NON-DENOMINATIONAL]
[SIMPLIFIED SERVICE FOR ALL CHRISTIAN DENOMINATIONS]

79

¶ *At the proper time and place appointed, the man and the woman to be married, having been qualified according to the laws of the State, shall stand facing the Minister [Chaplain], the man at the Chaplain's left hand, and the woman at his right hand.*

INTRODUCTION

¶ *The Chaplain addressing the company, shall say:*

We are gathered together here today in the presence of these witnesses, to unite _____ and _____ in marriage, which is ordained by the Church, sanctioned by the State, and made honourable by faithful keeping of good men and women of all ages. It is therefore not by any to be entered into lightly, but discreetly and with due reverence.

THE MARRIAGE SERVICE

¶ *The Chaplain, addressing the persons to be married, shall say:*

This celebration is an outward token of a sacred and inward union of hearts, which the Church may bless and the State make legal, but which neither can create. A union created by your loving purpose and kept by your abiding love. Into this estate you come now to be united.

Is it in this spirit and for this purpose that you have come hither to be joined together ?

¶ *Both the man and the woman shall answer:*

It is.

¶ *Then Chaplain shall continue, saying:*

I require and charge you both, as you stand in the presence of God that, having duly considered the holy covenant you are about to make, you do now declare before this company your pledge of faith, each to the other.

Be well assured that if these solemn vows are kept inviolet, as God's Word demands, and if steadfastly you endeavour to do the will of your heavenly Father, God will bless your marriage, will grant you fulfilment in it, and will establish your home in peace.

¶ *Then the Chaplain shall say:*

Who stands with this woman to symbolize the tradition and family from which she comes, to present her to be married to this man ?

¶ *The Bride's Father (or friend) shall answer:*

I do. [Alt: "Her Mother and I do"]

¶ *Then shall the Chaplain shall say unto the man:*

Will you, _____, take this woman to be your wife, to love and to cherish, to honour and to comfort, in sickness and in health, in sorrow and in joy, in hardship and in ease, to have and to hold, and to be faithful to her, from this day forth ?

¶ *Then the man shall answer:*

I will.

¶ *Then the Chaplain shall say unto the woman:*

Will you, _____, take this man to be your husband, to love and to cherish, to honour and to comfort, in sickness and in health, in sorrow and in joy, in hardship and in ease, to have and to hold, and to be faithful to him, from this day forth ?

¶ *The woman shall answer,*

I will.

¶ *Then the Chaplain shall cause the man with his right hand to take the woman by her right hand, and to say after him as follows:*

I, _____, take you _____, as my Wife, to have and to hold from this day forward, for better for worse, for richer for poorer, in sickness and in health, to love and to cherish, until death do us part; all this I promise to you, as God is my witness.

¶ *Then shall they loose hands; and the woman with her right hand taking the man by his right hand shall say after the Chaplain:*

I, _____, take you _____, as my Husband, to have and to hold from this day forward, for better for worse, for richer for poorer, in sickness and in health, to love and to cherish, until death do us part; all this I promise to you, as God is my witness.

¶ *The Chaplain will now secure the Wedding Ring from the 'Best Man' (or if two rings be used, from the 'Best Man' and the 'Maid of Honour' respectively) or from the Ring Bearer, and shall say:*

Bless, O Lord, the giving of these rings, that they who wear them may abide in thy peace, and continue in thy favour; through Jesus Christ our Lord.   Amen.

Or, if there be but one ring, the Chaplain may say:

Bless, O Lord, the giving of this Wedding Ring, that he who gives it and she who shall wear it may abide forever in thy peace, and continue in thy favour; through Jesus Christ our Lord.   Amen.

¶ *The Chaplain shall now deliver the Wedding Ring to the man to put upon the fourth finger of the woman's left hand.   The man, holding the ring there, shall say after the Chaplain:*

I give you this ring, in token and pledge of my constant faith and abiding love for you.

¶ *Then, if there is a Second Ring, the Chaplain shall deliver it to the woman to put upon the fourth finger of the man's left hand and the woman, holding it there, shall say after the Chaplain:*

I give you this ring, in token and pledge of my constant faith and abiding love for you.

¶ *If a Lesson from The Scriptures is to be included in the Service, then the Chaplain shall read from the First Letter of Paul to the Corinthians, Chapter 13, Verses 4-8 and 13, as follows:*

Love is patient; love is kind and envies no one. Love is never boastful, nor conceited, nor rude; never selfish, not quick to take offence. Love keeps no score of wrongs; does not gloat over other men's sins, but delights in the truth. There is nothing love cannot face; there is no limit to its faith, its hope, and its endurance. Love will never come to an end. There are three things that last forever: faith, hope, and love; but the greatest of them all is love.

¶ *Then shall the Chaplain join their right hands together and say,*

Those whom God hath joined together let no man put asunder !

¶ *Then shall the Chaplain speak unto the company,*

Since _____ and _____ have consented together in the bond of holy matrimony, and have pledged themselves each to the other, in the presence of God and these witnesses, by the power invested in me as a Minister of our Lord's Church, I pronounce that they are now lawfully married Husband and Wife.

¶ *Then the Chaplain may say unto the Man and his Wife:*   [Optional]

Now you will feel no rain, for each of you will be shelter for the other; Now you will feel no cold, for each of you will be warmth for the other; Now there will be no more loneliness, for though you are two persons, there is only one life before you. Go now to your dwelling place and enter into the days of your life together.

¶ *Then the Chaplain shall add this Blessing,*

God bless, preserve, and keep you; the Lord mercifully with His favour look upon you, and so fill you with all spiritual benediction and grace; that you may so live together in this life, that in the world to come you may have life everlasting. AMEN.

PRESENTATION

Ladies and Gentlemen, I now have the honour to present to you:

MR. AND MRS. _____.

THE MARRIAGE SERVICE
[SOLEMNIZATION OF HOLY MATRIMONY]
THE ORDER FOR MARRIAGE
[NON-DENOMINATIONAL]
[SIMPLIFIED 'SEMI-FORMAL' SERVICE FOR ALL CHRISTIAN DENOMINATIONS]

¶ *At the proper time and place appointed, the man and the woman to be married, having been qualified according to the laws of the State and the standards of the Church, shall stand facing the Minister [Chaplain], the man at the Chaplain's left hand, and the woman at his right hand.*

INTRODUCTION

¶ *The Chaplain addressing the company, shall say:*

Ladies and gentlemen, Greetings. Welcome to this happy and most important occasion for our friends _____ and _____.

Before we commence with the formal proceedings for which we are met here today, I have a few words of wisdom to impart to the Bride and 'Groom.

¶ *Then, addressing the persons to be married, he shall say:*

This rite of Marriage in which you now come to be united is the first and oldest rite of mankind. Marriage is our foretaste of paradise, given in the wisdom of God to soothe the troubles and to increase the joys of earthly life. This it will do for you, if you purpose in your hearts to beautify and sweeten it by your tender devotions, your mindfulness in little things, your patience and your sacrifice of self to each other. Coming in full love to the threshold of a new life together, I commend to you these spiritual ministries as the way of lasting happiness.

THE MARRIAGE SERVICE

¶ *The Chaplain, addressing the company, shall say:*

Dearly beloved, we are gathered together here in the sight of God, and in the presence of these witnesses, to join together this man and this woman in Holy Matrimony. It is an honourable estate, instituted by God for the comfort and help of his children and that families might be trained in goodness and godliness of life. Christ honoured it, sanctioned it, and beautified it both by his presence and solemn words. It is therefore not to be entered into unadvisedly or lightly; but reverently, discreetly, advisedly, soberly, and in the fear of God.

¶ *Then the Chaplain, addressing the persons to be married, shall say:*

I require and charge you both, that, having duly considered the holy covenant you are about to make, you do now declare before this company your pledge of faith, each to the other. Be assured that if these solemn vows are kept inviolet, as God's Word demands, and if steadfastly you endeavour to do the will of our heavenly Father, God will bless your marriage, will grant you fulfilment in it, and will establish your home in peace.

¶ *Then shall the Minister shall say unto the man:*

_____, Wilt thou have this woman to thy wedded wife, to live together in the holy estate of Matrimony ?   Wilt thou love her, comfort her, honour, and keep her in sickness and in health;   and, forsaking all others, keep thee only unto her, so long as ye both shall live ?

¶ *Then the man shall answer:*

I will.

¶ *Then the Chaplain shall say unto the woman:*

_____, Wilt thou have this man to thy wedded husband, to live together in the holy estate of Matrimony ?   Wilt thou [*be loyal unto him*], love, honour, and keep him, in sickness and in health;   and forsaking all others, keep thee only unto him, so long as ye both shall live ?

¶ *The woman shall answer,*

I will.

¶ *Then the Chaplain shall say,*

Who giveth this woman to be married to this man ?

¶ *The father of the woman (or whomsoever shall give her in marriage) shall answer:*

I do.

¶ *Then the Chaplain, receiving the woman at her father's (or friend's) hand, shall cause the man with his right hand to take the woman by her right hand, and to say after him as follows:*

I, _____, take thee _____, to my wedded Wife, to have and to hold from this day forward, for better for worse, for richer for poorer, in sickness and in health, to love and to cherish, 'till death us do part, according to God's holy ordinance; and thereto I pledge to thee my fidelity.

¶ *Then shall they loose hands;   and the woman with her right hand taking the man by his right hand shall say after the Chaplain:*

I, _____, take thee _____, to my wedded Husband, to have and to hold from this day forward, for better for worse, for richer for poorer, in sickness and in health, to love, [*and to*] cherish, [*and be loyal unto thee*], 'till death us do part, according to God's holy ordinance;   and thereto I give thee my fidelity.

¶ *The Chaplain will now secure the Wedding Ring from the 'Best Man' (or if two rings be used, from the 'Best Man' and the Maid of Honour respectfully) or from the Ring Bearer, and shall say:*

The Wedding Ring is the outward and visible sign of an inward and spiritual grace, signifying to all the uniting of this man and this woman in holy matrimony.

In the providence of God, and for the fullest happiness of the home, there are ways in which the Husband is the Head of the Wife. He imparts unto her his name, and receives her into his care and protection - in token of which he gives her this ring in pledge.

Thus are you, _____, [Bridegroom] to compass about her life with strength and protecting love. Thus are you, _____, [Bride] to wear this ring as the enclosing bond of reverence and dearest faith - both fulfilling the perfect circle of duty that makes you one.

¶ *Then the Chaplain may say:*

Bless, O Lord, the giving of these rings, that they who wear them may abide in thy peace, and continue in thy favour unto their life's end; through Jesus Christ our Lord. Amen.

Or, if there be but one ring, the Chaplain may say:

Bless, O Lord, the giving of this Wedding Ring, that he who gives it and she who shall wear it may abide forever in thy peace, and continue in thy favour; through Jesus Christ our Lord. Amen.

¶ *The Chaplain shall now deliver the Wedding Ring to the man to put upon the fourth finger of the woman's left hand. The man, holding the ring there, shall say after the Chaplain:*

In token and pledge of my constant faith and abiding love for you, with this ring I thee wed, [*with my body I thee worship and with all my worldly goods I thee endow*], as God is my witness. **Amen.**

¶ *Then, if there is a Second Ring, the Chaplain shall say:*

Because the man becomes to the woman her companion in all of life's experience, and is henceforth distinguished by his devotion to her, he wears this ring as the mark of his faithfulness.

¶ *The Chaplain now delivers the Second Ring to the woman to put upon the fourth finger of the man's left hand and the woman, **holding it there**, shall say after the Chaplain:*

In token and pledge of my constant faith and abiding love for you, with this ring I thee wed, as God is my witness. **Amen.**

¶ *If a Lesson from The Scriptures is to be included in the Service, then the Chaplain shall quote from the First Letter of Paul to the Corinthians, Chapter 13, Verses 4-8 and 13, as follows:*

Love is patient; love is kind and envies no one. Love is never boastful, nor conceited, nor rude; never selfish, not quick to take offence. Love keeps no score of wrongs; does not gloat over other men's sins, but delights in the truth. There is nothing love cannot face; there is no limit to its faith, its hope, and its endurance. Love will never come to an end.

There are three things that last forever: faith, hope, and love; but the greatest of them all is love. Praise be to God.

¶ Then the Chaplain shall say,

Let us Pray.

*Then shall the Chaplain **and the people**, still standing, **say the Lord's Prayer**.*

Our Father, who art in heaven, Hallowed be thy Name. Thy kingdom come. Thy will be done, On earth as it is in heaven. Give us this day our daily bread. And forgive us our trespasses, As we forgive them that trespass against us. And lead us not into temptation, But deliver us from evil. For thine is the kingdom, and the power, and the glory, for ever and ever. Amen.

¶ Then shall the Chaplain add,

O Eternal God, Creator and Preserver of all mankind, Giver of all spiritual grace, the Author of everlasting life; Send thy blessing upon these thy servants, this man and this woman, whom we bless in thy Name, that they, living faithfully together, may surely perform and keep the vow and covenant betwixt them made, and may ever remain in perfect love and peace together, and live according to thy laws; through Jesus Christ our Lord. Amen.

¶ Then shall the Chaplain join their right hands together and say,

Those whom God hath joined together let no man put asunder,

¶ Then shall the Chaplain speak unto the company,

Forasmuch as _____ and _____ have consented together in holy wedlock, witnessed this before God and this company, and thereto have given and pledged their fidelity, each to the other, and have so declared by joining hands and by giving and receiving a Ring; I pronounce that they are now Husband and Wife.

¶ Then the Chaplain shall say unto the Man and his Wife:

Now you will feel no rain, for each of you will be shelter for the other; Now you will feel no cold, for each of you will be warmth for the other; Now there will be no more loneliness, for though you are two persons, there is only one life before you. Go now to your dwelling place and enter into the days of your life together.

¶ Then the Chaplain shall add this Blessing,

God bless, preserve, and keep you; the Lord mercifully with His favour look upon you, and so fill you with all spiritual benediction and grace; that you may so live together in this life, that in the world to come you may have life everlasting. AMEN.

PRESENTATION

Ladies and Gentlemen, friends, I now have the honour to present to you:

MR. AND MRS. _____.

A CONTEMPORARY SHORT SERVICE

This, as is indicated by the heading to this chapter, is a very simple, and short service which you may find useful upon occasions where there may be little or no time for an actual interview as such - although hopefully at least some discussion over the telephone with the couple beforehand - and/or where, for one reason or another, it is only such a short marriage service that is required.

You may, for example, sometime be requested to perform a marriage for a couple who have been living together and where, one of them is seriously ill - maybe even terminally ill - and they're anxious to be married without delay.   And by reason of the patient's serious condition, unable to stand the stress of even a relatively simplified Order of Service.

In the event of one of the parties being so ill (or otherwise disabled) as to be unable to stand, or to kneel, during the marriage service;   then the minister can of course in his own discretion, further modify both the instructions and content of the service, accordingly.

For example, providing only that there shall be at least one witness [i. e. to sign the Marriage Licence & Certificate afterwards, along with the Minister also] - you may delete all but the most basic essentials and proceed simply as follows:

¶ *The Chaplain, addressing the persons to be married, shall say:*

This celebration is an outward token of a sacred and inward union of hearts, which the Church may bless and the State make legal, but which neither can create.   A union created by your loving purpose and kept by your abiding love.   Into this Holy estate you come now to be united.

¶ *Then shall the Chaplain shall say unto the man:*

Do you, _____, take this woman to be your wife, to love and to cherish, to honour and to comfort, in sickness and in health, in sorrow and in joy, in hardship and in ease, to have and to hold, and to be faithful to her, according to God's law, from this day forth ?

¶ *Then the man shall answer:*

I **do.**

¶ *Then the Chaplain shall say unto the woman:*

Do you, _____, take this man to be your husband, to love and to cherish, to honour and to comfort, in sickness and in health, in sorrow and in joy, in hardship and in ease, to have and to hold, and to be faithful to him, according to God's law, from this day forth ?

¶ *The woman shall answer,*

I **do.**

¶ *Then shall the Chaplain join their right hands together and say,*

Those whom God hath joined together let no man put asunder !

¶ *Then shall the Chaplain say,*   [Optional]

Since _____ and _____ have consented together in the bond of matrimony, and have pledged themselves each to the other, in the presence of God *and this/these witness(es)*, therefore by the power 'vested in me as a Minister of the Gospel, I pronounce that they are now lawfully Man and Wife.   May God bless this Marriage.

¶ *Then the Chaplain shall add this Blessing,*   [Optional]

God bless, preserve, and keep you;   the Lord mercifully with his favour look upon you, and so fill you with all spiritual benediction and grace, that you may so live together in this life, that in the world to come you may have life everlasting.   AMEN.

You will observe that in the above most brief marriage service, there is no provision for the woman to be 'given away' and, no provision for the giving and receiving of any ring(s).

If the man has available and wishes to give the woman a ring, this may be included in the marriage - taking the wording for his giving her a Wedding Ring (as also your Blessing of the ring) - from any of the other Orders of Service in this book.

In *California* [only] if the couple have only a *'Confidential Licence'*, then there need not even be a witness in attendance - since only the Officiating Minister [or Judge, or other person authorized to perform marriages] is required to sign in certification of the marriage.   That is to say, in addition to the couple themselves upon obtaining the Licence.

Thus in any real *emergency* situation, where 'time is of the essence' - then providing only that such a (valid) Licence can first be provided to the minister - he can perform the marriage, anywhere, instantly, and without anyone else being present at all.

¶ *At the proper time and place appointed, the man and the woman to be married, having been qualified according to the laws of the State, shall stand facing the Chaplain [Minister], the man at the Chaplain's left hand, and the woman at his right hand.*

INTRODUCTION

¶ *The Chaplain addressing the company, shall say:*

We are gathered together here today in the presence of these witnesses, to unite _____ and _____ in marriage, which is ordained by the Church, sanctioned by the State, and made honourable by faithful keeping of good men and women of all ages. It is therefore not by any to be entered into unadvisedly, or lightly, but discreetly and with due reverence.

THE MARRIAGE SERVICE

¶ *The Chaplain, addressing the persons to be married, shall say:*

This celebration is an outward token of a sacred and inward union of hearts, which the Church may bless and the State make legal, but which neither can create. A union created by your loving purpose and kept by your abiding love. Into this Holy estate you come now to be united.

¶ *Then the Chaplain shall say:*   [Optional]

Who stands with this woman to symbolize the tradition and family from which she comes, to present her to be married to this man ?

¶ *The Bride's Father (or friend) shall answer:*

I do.   [Alt: "Her mother and I do."]

¶ *Then shall the Chaplain shall say unto the man:*

Do you, _____, take this woman to be your wife, to love and to cherish, to honour and to comfort, in sickness and in health, in sorrow and in joy, in hardship and in ease, to have and to hold, and to be faithful to her, according to God's law, from this day forth ?

¶ *Then the man shall answer:*

I do.

¶ *Then the Chaplain shall say unto the woman:*

Do you, _____, take this man to be your husband, to love and to cherish, to honour and to comfort, in sickness and in health, in sorrow and in joy, in hardship and in ease, to have and to hold, and to be faithful to him, according to God's law, from this day forth ?

¶ *The woman shall answer,*

     I do.

¶ *Then the Chaplain shall ask of the man:*

_____, what pledge do you offer in token of your love for this woman ?

¶ *The man shall answer, producing a Wedding Ring to the Chaplain:*

     This ring.

¶ *The Chaplain shall cause the man to put the Wedding Ring on the fourth finger of the woman's left hand and to repeat after him as follows:*

     With this Ring I now marry you, and do pledge my constant and faithful love for you, as God is my witness.

¶ *Then, if two rings be used, the Chaplain shall similarly ask of the woman:*

_____, what pledge do you offer in token of your love for this man ?

¶ *The woman shall answer, producing a ring to the Chaplain:*

     This ring.

¶ *The Chaplain shall cause the woman to put the Ring on the fourth finger of the man's left hand and to repeat after him as follows:*

     With this Ring I now marry you, and do pledge my constant and faithful love for you, as God is my witness.

¶ *Then the Chaplain may say:*   [Optional]

     Bless, O Lord, the giving of these rings, that they who wear them may abide in thy peace, and continue in thy favour, through Jesus Christ our Lord.   Amen.

     Or, if there be but one ring, the Chaplain may say: [Optional]

     Bless, O Lord, the giving of this Wedding Ring, that he who gives it and she who wears it may abide forever in thy peace, and continue in thy favour, through Jesus Christ our Lord.   Amen.

¶ *Then shall the Chaplain join their right hands together and say,*

     Those whom God hath joined together let no man put asunder !

¶ *Then shall the Chaplain speak unto the company,*

     Since _____ and _____ have consented together in the bond of matrimony, and have pledged themselves each to the other, in the presence of God and these witnesses, therefore by the power 'vested in me as a Minister of the Gospel, I pronounce that they are now lawfully married Husband and Wife.   May God bless this Marriage.

¶ *Then the Chaplain may say unto the Man and his Wife:*

Now you will feel no rain, for each of you will be shelter for the other; Now you will feel no cold, for each of you will be warmth for the other; Now there will be no more loneliness, for though you are two persons, there is only one life before you. Go now to your dwelling place and enter into the days of your life together.

------------------------------------OPTIONAL------------------------------------

¶ *Then the Man and the Wife kneeling, the Chaplain shall add this Blessing,*

God bless, preserve, and keep you; the Lord mercifully with his favour look upon you, and so fill you with all spiritual benediction and grace, that you may so live together in this life, that in the world to come you may have life everlasting. AMEN.

PRESENTATION

Friends, I now have the honour to present to you:

MR. AND MRS. _____.

N. 3.

A CIVIL MARRIAGE CEREMONY

My own background is such that, just as (such as) a Registrar of Marriages, Commissioner or Judge (or whomsoever else among the Civil Authority) should not presume to perform a marriage using a Religious Service - neither should a Minister perform Secular Marriages.

This reminds me of a Notice in a Butcher's Shop in England which reads as follows:

> "We have an understanding with our Bank. They have agreed with us not to sell meat, and we have agreed with them not to cash cheques !"

In the United States of America, however, the Laws allow ministers to perform all marriages - irrespective of whether they do so by means of a Religious Service or simply with a Secular Ceremony.

If you feel inclined and prepared to officiate in Civil Marriages, you may find the 'Civil Wedding Ceremony' set down in this chapter, a useful guide.

Personally, I have only in a very few exceptional circumstances performed a Secular Marriage Ceremony - and I certainly will not officiate in a secular marriage - if it is required by reason of one or other of the parties being an atheist.

Beware.   You may have couples who will have the audacity to approach you as a minister, to perform a marriage - for no better reason than they know that, under the laws of the State, you are authorized to perform marriages. In short, simply because they are unable to find a Judge (or some other authorized official) prepared to come out to their chosen venue for their Wedding, rather than their having to go to him !

For all 'Civil Weddings' - check the couple's reasons for wanting only a secular ceremony and, their motivation in coming to you as a minister, to perform the marriage.

Although the minimal essential words are all that are legally required [see Chapter One] and a couple can become married within as little as fifteen seconds - it is in any case somewhat difficult to make very much of a Civil Ceremony for Matrimony - the ceremony provided herein does at least attempt to provide a meaningful 'ceremony' for the couple.   Once again using my favourite 'Scottish Poem' to so nicely round off the proceedings !

ORDER FOR MARRIAGE
[CONTEMPORARY]
[FOR PERSONS WHO *DO NOT* WANT A RELIGIOUS SERVICE FOR MATRIMONY]

¶ *At the proper time and place appointed, the man and the woman to be married, having been qualified according to the laws of the State, shall stand facing the Chaplain, the man at the Chaplain's left hand, and the woman at his right hand.*

INTRODUCTION

¶ *The Chaplain addressing the company, shall say:*

We are gathered together here to participate in the joining together of this man and this woman in Matrimony. What we do today is done in conformity to the laws of this State, and in the tradition of men and women of all places and all times. Marriage is also a Civil Ceremony, not surprisingly, with its dual origin in law and in sentiment.

This celebration is an outward token of an inward union of hearts, which a Church may bless and a State make legal, but which neither can create. A union created by loving purpose and kept by abiding love. Into this estate these two persons come now to be united.

THE MARRIAGE CEREMONY

¶ *The Chaplain, addressing the persons to be married, using their Full (Given and Last) Names, shall say:*

_____ and _____; you stand before me having requested that I marry you. I trust that you have given serious thought and consideration to the responsibilities you are both about to assume ?

¶ *Both the Bride and the 'Groom shall reply:*

We have.

¶ *Then the Chaplain shall say:*

Who stands with this Bride to represent the family from which she comes, and presents her to be married to this man ?

¶ *The Bride's Father [or friend] shall answer:*

I do.

¶ *Then shall the Chaplain cause the man and the woman to join hands, and he shall say to the man, using both his and the woman's Full (Given and Last) Names:*

Do you, _____, take _____ for your lawful wife ? Do you promise to love and sustain her in marriage from this day forward, in sickness and in health, in plenty and in want, in joy and in sorrow, until death do you part ?

¶ *Then the man shall answer:*

I do.

¶ *Then the Chaplain shall say unto the woman, using both hers and the man's Full (Given and Last) Names:*

Do you, _____ take _____ for your lawful husband ? Do you promise to love and sustain him in marriage from this day forward, in sickness and in health, in plenty and in want, in joy and in sorrow, until death do you part ?

¶ *The woman shall answer,*

I do.

¶ *The Chaplain will now secure the Wedding Ring and shall say:*

The Wedding Ring is the outward and visible symbol of your marriage — symbolic of the fact that you have this day pledged yourselves in marriage; and as the ring is a perfect circle without end, it is the wish and hope of all that your marriage will be as perfect and without end.

-------------------------------OPTIONAL-------------------------------------

For the fullest happiness of the home, there are ways in which the Husband is the Head of the Wife. He imparts unto her his name, and receives her into his care and protection - in token of which he gives her this ring in pledge.

Thus are you, _____, ['Groom] to compass about her life with strength and protecting love. Thus are you, _____, [Bride] to wear this ring as the enclosing bond of dearest love, fulfilling the perfect circle of duty that makes you one.

¶ *The Chaplain shall now deliver the Wedding Ring to the man to put upon the fourth finger of the woman's left hand. The man, **holding the ring there**, shall say after the Chaplain:*

With this ring I thee **wed**, giving it as a token and pledge of **my** abiding love for you.

-------------------------------OPTIONAL-------------------------------------

¶ *Then, the Chaplain shall secure the Second Ring and shall say:*

Because the man becomes to the woman her companion in all of life's experience, and is henceforth distinguished by his devotion to her, he wears this ring as the mark of his faithfulness.

¶ *The Chaplain now delivers the Second Ring to the woman to put upon the fourth finger of the man's left hand and the woman, **holding it there**, shall say after the Chaplain:*

With this ring I thee wed, giving it as a token and pledge of my abiding love for you.

¶ *Then shall the Chaplain speak unto the company,*

Since _____ and _____ have consented together in marriage, and have declared the same before us by pledging their love, each to the other, and by joining hands, by the authority 'vested in me by the State, I pronounce that they are now lawfully married Husband and Wife.

¶ *Then the Chaplain may say unto the Man and his Wife:*

Now you will feel no rain, for each of you will be shelter for the other; Now you will feel no cold, for each of you will be warmth for the other; Now there will be no more loneliness, for though you are two persons, there is only one life before you. Go now to your dwelling place and enter into the days of your life together.

PRESENTATION

Ladies and Gentlemen, I now have the honour to present to you:

MR. AND MRS. _____.

--C. 1.

A REAFFIRMATION SERVICE

An husband and wife do not have to wait until their Silver Wedding (or any
other particular anniversary) to Reaffirm their Vows - I have had couples
renew their vows on their tenth, fifth, even first anniversary of their
marriage.   Indeed, quite a number do so on their first anniversary, and a
few do so on almost every anniversary !

Usually, it's a quiet little gathering of close family and friends in their
own home - except for such as a 'Silver' or 'Gold', at which times they'll
have a full-scale celebration [e.g. "Silver Wedding and Reception"] at some
suitable venue, much the same as for any regular Wedding.

Just as long as you are only performing a *Reaffirmation* Service and not an
actual *marriage* as such - and thus *not* issuing a Marriage Certificate to
mark the occasion - you have no need to be concerned about licences.

However, if you do wish to verify when, where and by whom they were married
- checking to see if by a member of the clergy or by a civil authority or
official - you might care to ask them for a photo-copy of their original
licence (and/or marriage certificate) for your files.

In cases where they cannot remember exactly how their vows were worded, you
can discuss with them how they would now like to 'reaffirm' (or maybe even
'up-grade') their vows !

You will sometimes find that the couple had what was, in effect, really
only a Civil Ceremony - as there were no (religious) vows made - only the
legally required undertaking to accept each other as man and wife.   In such
cases, one cannot 'renew' vows that were never made in the first place !
Thus for them, it will not be a Reaffirmation Service that you'll be giving
them, but instead performing an actual marriage service.

Some time ago I had just such a case which generated considerable amusement
in the family concerned.   A young couple came to me requesting that I
officiate at their wedding.   Upon later learning that the bride's grandparents (on her mother's side) were to celebrate their 'Golden Wedding
Anniversary' at roughly the same time - with family and friends attending
from far and wide who had not had any opportunity to meet together for
many, many years - they decided to co-ordinate the two events to take place
on the same day at the same venue.   This was going to be quite an event.

Subsequently however, the bride's mother remembered her mother having once
confessed to her that she had only had a Civil Ceremony, and that they had
never followed this up with a religious service.   In short, the couple had
been legally married for fifty years "in the eyes of the State" - but not
as yet also "before God."   Accordingly, they could not have a Reaffirmation
Service as such;   it would have to be a Marriage Service - albeit fifty
years late.

The bride's mother then asked me if I would therefore be asking her
father: "Wilt thou have this woman to thy wedded wife....etc.?" and
when I replied in the affirmative, she exclaimed: "Good heavens, I'm
forty-eight years old now - what if he were to say 'No' ?"

Following in this chapter is an example of a basic 'Reaffirmation Service' that I use - and in fact adapt in minor detail as necessary to suit each case.   This one is of course suitable - and easy to fill in the gaps - if the couple originally had the 'Traditional' Marriage Service and, you know exactly what their vows were, when and where, having performed the marriage for them yourself.

On the other hand, if the couple cannot remember what their vows were, and not having performed their marriage yourself, you have no record of it, you may suggest re-wording part of the service, to read as follows:

¶ *Then the Chaplain shall say unto the Husband and his Wife:*

"The vows that you are about to make in reaffirmation to each other now, may not be be in precisely the same wording in which you made them on your actual Wedding Day - the words you'll be using now, are those that have been used through many Centuries past in Christian Church, and are still used today in any 'Traditional' Solemnization of Holy Matrimony."

And if they know that their original vows did not include the 'obey' and so forth, they might wish to 'up-grade' them - and include this now.

As an example of how one can so easily personalize a Reaffirmation Service for a couple, here follows my opening address [but with names changed] for one couple celebrating their Thirtieth Wedding Anniversary:

¶ *The Chaplain, addressing the company, shall say,*

"We are here today for the most joyful occasion of witnessing two of our friends who, upon celebrating their **THIRTIETH WEDDING ANNIVERSARY**, wish now to reaffirm their vows, and in so doing, confirming their continued devotion and love for each other.

I may add that not only is the actual anniversary of their **WEDDING DAY** next Monday, but it was **JOHN'S BIRTHDAY** last Monday - and it will be **JANE'S FIFTIETH BIRTHDAY**, next Thursday !   This week-end is therefore indeed a most opportune moment for celebration with their family and friends, many of whom have come here today from several distant lands.

The Service of Solemnization of Holy Matrimony is a moving experience for all who participate in it;   it is one which many feel they would like to share with their partners in life again; And there's no reason why they should not do so; indeed, just as it is always comforting and reassuring to have one's partner say again and again "I love you", it is certain that God must be happy to witness the event of two of His children repeating their Marriage Vows to each other as well.

This is not of course to be another Marriage Service as such, since for this couple, that took place in the **Church of St. Michael and All Saints, Little Ilford in the County of Essex, England**, some thirty years ago.   It will nevertheless include their original vows, reminding them of what then took place - when they first set sail on the Sea of Matrimony together. "

Fortunately, in this case they still had a recording of their marriage in that church, and were therefore able to check this and repeat their vows verbatim.   Being the 'Traditional' (Original) version, I'm pleased to say.

¶ *At a proper time and place the Husband and Wife shall stand facing the Chaplain [Minister], the man at the Chaplain's left hand, and the woman at his right hand.*

INTRODUCTION

¶ *The Chaplain, addressing the company, shall say,*

We are here today for the most joyful occasion of witnessing two of our friends who, being already happily married, wish now to reaffirm their vows, and in so doing, confirm their continued devotion and love for each other.

The Service of Solemnization of Holy Matrimony is a moving experience for all who participate in it; it is one which many feel they would like to share with their partners in life – again.   And there is no reason why they should not do so;   indeed, just as it is always comforting and reassuring to have one's partner say again and again "I love you", it is certain that God must also be happy to witness the event of two of His children repeating their Marriage Vows to each other.

This is not of course to be another Marriage Service as such, since for this couple, that took place at _____, in the City of _____, on _____.   It will nevertheless include their original vows, reminding them of what then took place – when they first set sail on the Sea of Matrimony together.

ORDER OF SERVICE

¶ *Then the Chaplain shall say,*

In the Name of the Father, and of the Son, and of the Holy Ghost.   Amen.

¶ *Then addressing the company, he shall say:*

Dearly beloved, we are gathered together here in the sight of God, and in the face of this company, to witness this man and this woman renew and reaffirm their vows in Holy Matrimony, an honourable estate, instituted by God, signifying unto us the mystical union that is betwixt Christ and his Church. The holy estate which Christ adorned and beautified with his presence and first miracle that he wrought in Cana of Galilee, and which is commended of St. Paul to be honourable among all men, and therefore not by any to be entered into unadvisedly or lightly; but reverently, discreetly, advisedly, soberly, and in the fear of God.

¶ *Then addressing the Husband, he shall say,*

_____, Wilt thou continue in your commitment to this woman, your wedded wife, living together after God's ordinance in the holy estate of Matrimony ?   Wilt thou continue to love her, comfort her, honour and keep her, in sickness and in health, and forsaking all other, still keep thee only unto her, so long as ye both shall live ?

¶ *Then the Husband shall answer.*

I will.

¶ *Then the Chaplain shall say unto the Wife,*

_____, Wilt thou continue in your commitment to this man, your wedded husband, living together after God's ordinance in the holy estate of matrimony ? Wilt thou continue to obey him, and serve him, love, honour and keep him, in sickness and in health, and forsaking all other, still keep thee only unto him, so long as ye both shall live ?

¶ *Then the Wife shall answer,*

I will.

THE VOWS

¶ *Then the Chaplain shall say unto the Husband and his Wife:*

The vows that you are about to make in reaffirmation to each other now, are in precisely the same wording in which you made them on your actual Wedding Day - they are words that have been used through many Centuries past in the Christian Church, in any 'Traditional' Solemnization of Holy Matrimony.

[To the Husband] Now, _____, take _____'s right hand in your right hand, and in confirmation that you will continue to uphold your marriage vows, repeat these words after me:

¶ *The Husband shall now say after the Chaplain:*

I, _____, take thee, _____, to my wedded wife, to have and to hold from this day forward, for better for worse, for richer for poorer, in sickness and in health, to love and to cherish, 'till death us do part, according to God's holy ordinance; and thereto I plight thee my troth.

[To the Wife] Now, _____, take _____'s right hand in your right hand, and in confirmation that you will continue to uphold your marriage vows, repeat these words after me:

¶ *The Wife shall now say after the Chaplain:*

I, _____, take thee, _____, to my wedded husband, to have and to hold from this day forward, for better for worse, for richer for poorer, in sickness and in health, to love, cherish and to obey, 'till death us do part, according to God's holy ordinance; and thereto I give thee my troth.

THE WEDDING RING(S)

¶ *The Chaplain shall now say:*

In the providence of God, and for the fullest happiness of the home, there are ways in which the husband is the head of the wife. He imparts unto her his name, and receives her into his care and protection - in token of which he gives her a Ring in pledge.

This you, _____, did for your wife when you were joined together in Marriage just _____ year(s) ago today; and thus you did compass about her life with strength and protecting love.

And thus you _____, are wearing his Ring as the enclosing bond of reverence and dearest faith, both fulfilling the perfect circle of duty that makes you one. The Wedding Ring should of course never have had occasion to be removed from your hand, and I do not propose that you should remove it now – not even so that your husband may present it to you afresh. However, he can nevertheless say the traditional undertaking that is made by a Bridegroom when giving a Wedding Ring to his Bride during their Marriage Ceremony – and I now invite him so to do..

¶ *The Husband shall* **take hold of** *the Wedding Ring on the fourth finger of his wife's left hand, and shall say after the Chaplain:*

With this ring I thee wed, *with my body I thee worship, and with all my worldly goods I thee endow,* **in the Name of the Father, and of the Son, and of the Holy Ghost. Amen.**

¶ *Then the Chaplain shall say:*

Because the man becomes to the woman her companion in all of life's experience, and is distinguished by his devotion to her, he also wears her Ring as the mark of his faithfulness. I invite her also to say now the traditional words used by a Bride when in her turn giving a Ring to her Bridegroom during their Wedding Ceremony.

¶ *The Wife shall now* **take hold of** *the Ring on the fourth finger of her husband's left hand, and shall say after the Chaplain:*

With this ring I thee wed, in the Name of the Father, and of the Son, and of the Holy Ghost. Amen.

¶ *Then, placing his hands upon their (ring) hands, the Chaplain* **may** *say:*

Bless, O Lord, these rings, that they who wear them may abide in thy peace, and continue in thy favour, unto their life's end; through Jesus Christ our Lord. Amen.

THE LESSON

¶ *Then the Chaplain may say:*

The Lesson is taken from the First Letter of Paul to the Corinthians, Chapter 13., Verses 4 to 8 and 13.

Love is patient, love is kind and envies no one. Love is never boastful, nor conceited, nor rude; never selfish, not quick to take offence. Love keeps no score of wrongs; does not gloat over other men's sins, but delights in the truth. There is nothing love cannot face; there is no limit to its faith, its hope, and its endurance. Love will never come to an end.

There are three things that last forever: faith, hope, and love; but the greatest of them all is love. Praise be to God.

PRAYERS

¶ *Then the Chaplain shall say,*

Let us pray.

¶ *Then shall the Chaplain* **and the people** *still standing,* **say the Lord's Prayer,**

Our Father, which art in heaven, Hallowed be thy Name. Thy Kingdom come. Thy will be done, On earth as it is in heaven. Give us this day our daily bread. And forgive us our trespasses, As we forgive them that trespass against us. And lead us not into temptation, But deliver us from evil. For thine is the kingdom, and the power, and the glory, for ever and ever. Amen.

¶ *Then shall the Chaplain add,*

O Eternal God, Creator and Preserve of all mankind, Giver of all spiritual grace, the Author of everlasting life; Send thy blessing upon these thy servants, this man and this woman, whom we bless in thy Name; that they, living faithfully together, may surely continue to perform and keep the vows and covenant betwixt them made, and may ever remain in perfect love and peace together, living according to thy laws; through Jesus Christ our Lord. Amen.

¶ *Then shall the Chaplain shall speak to the company,*

Remember ... Those whom God hath joined together, let no man put asunder !

and the Chaplain may add:

Perhaps, like many of us, you have experienced a few "ups and downs" in your marriage – and even if you have not – let me read for you a little Scottish Poem so appropriate for a marriage; and imagine that you are both about to 'start afresh' in life together......

[*addressing the Husband and Wife, the Chaplain shall continue as follows*]

Now you will feel no rain, for each of you will be shelter for the other; now you will feel no cold, for each of you will be warmth for the other. Now there will be no more loneliness; for 'though you are two persons, there is only one life before you. Go now to your dwelling place, and enter into the days of your life together.

THE BENEDICTION

¶ *Then the Man and Wife kneeling, the Chaplain shall add this Blessing,*

God the Father, God the Son, God the Holy Ghost, bless, preserve, and keep you; the Lord mercifully with his favour look upon you, and fill you with all spiritual benediction and grace; that ye may so continue to live together in this life, that in the world to come ye may have life everlasting. Amen.

PRESENTATION

Ladies and Gentlemen, I now have the honour to present to you, once again:

MR. & MRS. _____

_____ R.1.

SUPPLEMENTARY CEREMONIES

Either during the course of the Marriage Service, or, under certain circumstances, subsequently at the Wedding Reception; you may be required to (or
may care to suggest that you) include certain other 'ceremonies' as well.

The Candles Ceremony

During the Marriage Service; following the Prayers *and immediately prior
to your making the Declaration "Those whom God hath joined together, let no
man put asunder." the following insert may be made in the Service:*

   ¶ *Then the Minister shall say:*

   These two lighted candles represent the distinctly separate ways that
   you have been free to go until this day.   To bring bliss and
   happiness to your marriage, there must be the merging of these two
   lights into one light.   This is what our Lord meant when he said "On
   this account a man shall leave his mother and father and be joined to
   his wife and the two shall be one flesh."

   From this day forward, your thoughts and deeds shall be for each other
   rather than for your individual selves; your plans shall be mutual;
   your joys and sorrows shall be alike.

   As you each take a candle and together light the Wedding Candle, you
   will then extinguish your own candles - thus having this Unity Candle
   represent the union of your lives into one.   As this one light cannot
   be divided, neither shall your lives be divided, but henceforth
   evidence a testimony of your unity in our Lord Jesus Christ.

For this, the couple should ideally have a "Wedding Candles Set" [obtained
from a 'Gospel Book Shop' or any other good store specializing in accoutre-
ments for weddings] usually comprising one large thick 'Unity Candle' in
the center with a small thin candle at each side of it.   Alternatively, a
triple Candelabrum may suffice - with the center candle being highest or
longer than the others.

[At The Reception]

There will be occasions where it would be quite impossible to include the
'Candle Ceremony' in the actual Marriage Service.   For example, when it is
being held aboard a yacht, in a park, or elsewhere out of doors.   In such
cases, it could be desirable to have this later, as a *formal opening* to the
proceedings at the Reception instead.

As soon as the newly married couple have made their way to the 'Top Table',
the Minister, joining the couple where the Candelabrum is placed, should
call the assembled guests to order, requesting that they "be seated" - and
then proceed with the ceremony, reading exactly as set down above.
However, at the conclusion of that reading, turning to the assembled
company as a whole, *he may add:*

   "The Grace of our Lord Jesus Christ, the love of God, and the
   fellowship of the Holy Ghost, be with us all, evermore.   Amen."

The Wine Cup Ceremony

Also, upon occasions, you may be requested to include a "Wine Cup Ceremony" in the Marriage Service.   In such cases, the following is suggested for addition immediately following "The Benediction" [i.e. prior to making your Presentation of the man and his wife to the assembled congregation or company.]

¶   *Then shall the Minister say unto the Man and his Wife:*

Now may your first act in holy wedded life be an act of sharing.   This cup of wine is symbolic of the cup of life.   As you share in this one cup of wine, you agree to share all that the future may bring.   All the sweetness life's cup may hold for you should be the sweeter, because you drink it together;   whatever drops of bitterness it may contain, should be less bitter because you share them too.   As I say the Blessing over the wine, we all pray that God will grant you fullness of joy.

¶   *Then (upon handing the Cup of Wine, first to the Husband), the Minister shall say:*

God the Father, God the Son, God the Holy Ghost, we praise thee who creates the fruit of the vine a symbol of joy;   Bless, O Lord, this wine and these thy servants who now partake of it in thy Name.   Amen.

In the event of there being a desire [e.g. as in some Non-Denominational Services, or in a marriage between Jew and Christian] to avoid mention of the Holy Trinity - then the last paragraph should be changed to read:

Almighty God, we praise thee who creates the fruit of the vine a symbol of joy;   Bless O Lord this wine and these thy servants who now partake of it in thy Name.   Amen.

An Invocation at The Wedding Breakfast

Where you may be invited to attend the couple's Reception after the Service you may also be asked to say "grace" [i.e. thanksgiving before (or after) a meal] for all assembled thereat.   The following is suggested:

"O Thou to whom we owe the gift of life, the provisions for our care, the capacity to love, the support of family, and the joy of friendship: we express our gratitude for the "ties that bind our hearts to Thee in Christian love", through Jesus Christ, our Lord.   Amen.

Our God and Father, whose nature is love, we thank Thee for this happy hour that brings us together as family and friends of

_____ and _____.

As we share in food and fellowship honouring this couple, may we be mindful of the manifestations of Thy love.   Amen.

The Grace of the Lord Jesus Christ, the love of God, and the fellowship of the Holy Ghost be with us all, now and for evermore. Amen. "

SUPPLEMENTARY INFORMATION

Payment of Fees - at the time of the Interview

A minister having his own Parish Church, and marrying a couple where one or both of the parties are members of his congregation, invariably should not and will not charge any fee for performing the marriage - considering such of his ministerial duties to be part of his vocation for which he already receives a salary.   On the other hand it is traditional that the minister be given an appropriate monetary gift [Honorarium] as an expression of appreciation, usually by (or via) the Best Man - sometime shortly *after* he has performed the marriage.

In the case of any minister who does not have his own church and/or who does not receive any salary as such, and who may therefore have to depend upon fees for his services and expenses incurred performing marriages - he is entitled and indeed expected to require a fee for services provided to any couple having him officiate at their wedding.

The amount of the fee he may require is of course entirely within his own discretion, payable by the Bridegroom - preferably *in advance* at the time of the Interview.   It is also customary for someone [e.g. Bridegroom's father - or if he has already paid the basic fee for his son beforehand, then the Bridegroom (via the Best Man)] to present the minister with a suitable Honorarium shortly *after* the service *as well.*

Wedding Rehearsal

If the marriage is to be performed in a church or chapel, it is certainly advisable to arrange for a rehearsal, when all the parties concerned can be present.   Ideally, this should be early evening, the night before the Wedding.   Similarly, if to be held elsewhere, and a formal procedure is to be required in such as the seating of guests, bridegroom's parents and the bride's mother, the processional, and so forth.

The rehearsal will put everyone at ease when the time of the wedding arrives.   If there is to be a rehearsal dinner, it should be served after the rehearsal rather than before, when everyone will be more relaxed.

However, for most 'small weddings' and, most certainly those to take place aboard such as a yacht or other relatively small vessel to be chartered for the occasion - a rehearsal is hardly necessary, less still practicable.

It will invariably suffice for the minister to *briefly* advise the couple at the time of the interview (shortly after accepting their booking) as to what is to happen - and to arrive on the day of the wedding at least half-an-hour ahead of time to provide a *detailed* 'briefing' separately to each of the parties involved more-or-less 'on site' when they can hardly forget his instructions, given only moments before they are about to carry them out.

The minister should first call upon the bride, with her maid of honour and bridesmaids no doubt already in attendance with her, to determine who is to be in the Processional and to brief them on (i) the order of procession and (ii) how soon after the processional music starts, the first of them should move forward, and timing for each of the others to follow so that (iii) the bride and her father [or whoever] shall arrive at the designated place for the marriage, as the music reaches its finale.

The minister should then meet with the bride's father and instruct him as to his duties in the proceedings; then finally join with the bridegroom and 'best man' to brief them - and in due course make his entry with them.

The Wedding - Order of Procedure

The order of procedure for the Wedding will usually be as follows:

Preliminary Organ (or other suitable) Music
Arrival of the Guests
Seating of the Bridegroom's Parents and the Bride's Mother
The Minister
The Bridegroom and his Supporter [Best Man]
The Wedding March - Processional
The Bride's Party
The Marriage Ceremony
The Recessional

Depending upon the configuration of the surroundings [i.e. building or, if at sea, the vessel] the minister, bridegroom, his supporter ['Best Man'] should if possible enter from the right side, and await the arrival of the bride at the appointed place for the marriage - and the bride and her party to 'walk up the aisle' from the rear (between the rows of chairs set out for the guests) to her appointed place in front of the Minister.

In the United States, it appears general for the ushers to lead preceding the bridesmaids, followed by the maid (or matron) of honour, then the flower girl and ring bearer (if any) and finally, the bride and her father.

In the United Kingdom (and elsewhere in the British Commonwealth) it is quite the reverse - with the bride and her father leading the procession. [See Chapter XVI.]

It is also customary in some churches (in the United States) for the bride to be on her father's left arm - so that upon arrival at the altar or other appointed place for the marriage, he shall (initially) stand between her and the bridegroom.   Also that the ushers and bridesmaids stand more-or-less one behind the other - at each side, behind the bride and 'groom.

Personally, I prefer that the bride enter on her father's right arm, and remain between her and her attendants until I have received her at his hand [i.e. until he has "given her away"] following which he should then take his seat next to the bride's mother.   Also for the bridesmaids to form a line (after the maid of honour who remains nearest to the bride) stretching away to my right - and for the ushers to form a line (after the Best Man) stretching away to my left - all facing the altar.

Often, aboard a relatively small vessel at sea, it simply isn't possible to have the processional comprise ushers and/or bridesmaids marching in pairs - it being difficult enough for the bride and her father to walk side-by-side anyway.   In these circumstances, I have the bridegroom, best man, and the ushers (if any) all assemble at their appointed places with me from the outset - and have only the bride and her attendants make a processional; with all except for the bride and her father, approaching in single file.

Also, if aboard a small vessel at sea, with the marriage taking place at the foremast (or bow or stern) whilst I have the bride's father, the bride, and the bridegroom all facing me - I have their supporters stand either side of myself, with maid (or matron) of honour nearest to my right, and the 'best man' nearest to my left, facing inwards towards them and myself.

Frankly, there need be no hard and fast rules as to what form the processional should take.   Within reasonable bounds, this can be left to the personal preferences of the bride and 'groom working in liaison with the officiating minister.   The Recessional is in reverse order.

The Receiving Line after the Service

If the 'Receiving Line' is to be at the Reception - being at a different venue from the place of the marriage - then the Wedding Party must proceed ahead of their guests, and be assembled immediately inside the entrance of the room in which it is to be held.   The 'Receiving Line' may then be formed as follows:

Mother of the Bride
Father of the Bride
Mother of the 'Groom
Father of the 'Groom
Bride and Bridegroom
[*The Bride standing to the right of the 'Groom*]
Maid (or Matron) of Honour
The Bridegroom's Supporter ['Best Man']

The Fathers can, if so desired, be excused - to mingle with the guests and ensure that food service and entertainment is proceeding according to plan.

However, if the 'Receiving Line' is to be held immediately following the marriage and, at the same (informal) venue, such as aboard a vessel at sea; then it may only be possible for the Recessional (if any) to take the form of a 'walk around the deck' to some convenient place where 'the line' can be formed.

In the Recessional, the bride's father will be joined by her mother [from her front row seat nearest the 'aisle' on the bride's side of the congregation] to follow the maid (or matron) of honour, best man and other attendants;   followed by the bridegroom's mother and father [from their front row seats nearest the 'aisle' on his side of the congregation] with the chaplain [minister] bringing up the rear.

Divorced Parents

If the bride's parents and/or the bridegroom's parents happen to be divorced and either have later remarried - and their spouses are *also* in attendance at the Wedding - *none of these spouses* should, under any circumstances whatsoever, be in the line.   In fact, they should try to maintain as 'low a profile' as possible throughout the entire proceedings.

That is to say, excepting *only* in cases where (i) the actual mother or father is *not* also present [e.g. deceased] *and* (ii) such spouse has in fact been accepted, and has served as, an active step-mother or step-father in the rearing of the bride or 'groom (as the case may be) as a child.

This is an occasion when, regardless of their personal differences (if any) subsequent to their divorce;   the parents should put on a 'good face' at least throughout this day, and play their part as proud parents - and their later spouses' presence be [if necessary] purely coincidental.

There must be *no animosity in evidence at all* between any current and former wives of fathers, nor between any current and former husbands of mothers, who may find themselves in company together on this occasion.

Duties and Financial Obligations of the Bridegroom and/or his Parents

The bridegroom should purchase the Marriage Licence, the Wedding Ring, and pay the Minister.   And it goes without saying that it is for him to make all necessary arrangements, in advance, for the honeymoon.

His financial responsibilities are as follows:

> Bride's engagement and wedding rings
>
> Bride's wedding gift
>
> Gifts for his supporter [best man] and other attendants
>
> Marriage licence
>
> Physical examination [blood test, etc.]
>
> Minister's Fee [and later honorarium also if from none other]
>
> Hotel accommodations for his attendants from out of town
>
> Bride's bouquet and going-away corsage
>
> Corsages for the mothers and grandmothers of the bride and the 'groom
>
> Boutonnieres for all men in the wedding party - some suggest also for the Minister as well, but personally I would not agree with this.
>
> The Honeymoon.

His parents' financial responsibilities are as follows:

> Their own wedding clothes
>
> Their own travel expenses to and from the wedding
>
> Their own hotel accommodation
>
> Wedding gift for the bride and bridegroom
>
> Bachelor's dinner for their son and his supporters and friends
>
> Rehearsal dinner

Hotel accommodation for 'best man' and male attendants - if unable to accommodate them in their own home.

Duties and Financial Obligations of the Bride and/or her Parents

The sensible and practical bride will not insist upon an elaborate wedding, not least of all because the major portion of the wedding expenses (traditionally) fall upon her parents, but also because squandering of money upon any non-essential items is senseless - when it could be better spent on more durable things for her new home.

Fortunately, in the present day, it is not unusual for the 'groom and/or his family to assume part of the financial obligations.

However, allowing for all eventualities - traditionally, the Bride's own financial responsibilities are as follows:

Bridegroom's ring [if two rings are to be used]

Bridegroom's wedding gift

Maid (or Matron) of Honour's gift

Bridesmaids' gifts

Physical examination [blood test, etc.]

Her Parents' financial responsibilities are as follows:

Printing and mailing of Invitations, Cards and Announcements

Wedding gift for bride and bridegroom

Bride's gown, veil and accessories

Bride's trousseau

Bridesmaids' luncheon

Rental of the church and custodial fees - or alternative venue
[e.g. hotel ballroom, chartered yacht, etc.] for the Wedding.

Organist and soloist [if in church] or other musicians

Decorations [in the church, or elsewhere as the case may be]

Bridesmaids' bouquets

Wedding Reception - rental, catering, wedding cake, bar, music, decorations, flowers, gratuities, etc.

Engagement and Wedding portraits

Wedding and Reception photography; video, etc.

Transportation for the Bridal Party to and from the Church (or other designated place) for the Wedding and the Reception.

Hotel accommodation for maid (or matron) of honour and attendants - if unable to accommodate them in their own home.

Duties of the Maid (or Matron) of Honour

The maid (or matron) of honour, being the bride's most important attendant, is usually her sister or very best friend.   Next to the bride's parents, the maid of honour should be one of the first to be told about the Wedding and of her selection as maid of honour.   Preferably several months ahead of time, and certainly before the invitations are sent out, so that the date can be entered into her schedule and necessary arrangements can be made.

Unless the bride is able to afford it and, wishes to give her the wedding outfit, the maid of honour should be prepared to purchase her own wedding clothes.   The bride will nevertheless give her the flowers which she will be carrying.

The duties and responsibilities of the maid of honour are as follows:

Attend the Rehearsal (if any)

Arrange the bride's train (if any) as the procession forms up, and again at the altar if necessary;   and to straighten it out behind the bride as she turns around to make the recessional.

Hold the bride's bouquet during the exchange of rings

Carry the bridegroom's ring during the ceremony - unless there is a ring-bearer - and give it to the minister at the appropriate moment.

Assist the bride in changing clothes and packing for her honeymoon

Ensure that no 'tricks' in bad taste are played.

Duties of the Bridegroom's Supporter ['Best Man']

The 'best man', being the bridegroom's most important attendant, is usually his brother or very best friend.   He, like the maid of honour, must also be chosen and advised well in advance of the Wedding, so that he too can make whatever adjustments may be necessary in order to be present.

The primary duties of the 'best man' are as follows:

Aid the 'groom in every way he can in preparation for the wedding;   to protect him from pranks and, under no circumstances whatsoever partic-ipate in any practical jokes played upon the bride and 'groom.

Attend the Rehearsal (if any) and assist the minister in gaining the full co-operation of the male attendants - and to also ensure that all arrive in good time for the wedding.

Help the 'groom dress for the wedding and, go with him to the church (or wheresoever the marriage is to take place) to arrive there at least half-an-hour ahead of time.

Deliver the Marriage Licence to the minister;   when called upon to do so, to sign the licence and, to ensure that the maid of honour also shall sign as a witness to the marriage.

Give the minister his fee [in the event it has not already been paid in advance at Interview] and/or an appropriate honorarium [gratuity]

in appreciation of his services.   This should be given to him incon-
spicuously, in a plain white sealed envelope, as soon as conveniently
possible after he has performed the marriage.   *It should be more than
a mere '15% Tip'* [as if to a waiter] *since that would be derisive !*

Accompany the 'groom to the altar [or such alternative place as may be
assigned for the marriage]

Carry the bride's ring during the ceremony - unless there is a ring-
bearer - and give it to the minister at the appropriate moment.   If
the 'groom is wearing gloves, the 'best man' will hold them for him
during the ceremony.

If the Reception is to be elsewhere, he will fetch the hats and coats
of the bride and 'groom, meet them at the door, and chauffeur them
(and the maid of honour) to the reception.

Help the 'groom pack, take charge of the couple's baggage, seeing that it
is safely stowed in their car.   Keep safe the keys to the car and, when
it is time for them to depart, ensure that they get away safely.

Photographers

If the Wedding is to be in a church, the photographer should of course be
kept out of sight throughout the marriage service - being allowed to take
photos only of the processional and the recessional.

Where the Wedding is to take place in an informal atmosphere elsewhere;
whilst the minister might permit of a trustworthy photographer to take a
few photos (at a distance) of the processional, and during the course of
the actual service [e.g. the exchange of the rings], under no circumstances
whatsoever should any photographs be taken, by anyone at all, during
prayers.   When the minister says "Let us pray", that is precisely what he
expects everyone to be doing.   The 'clicking' of cameras, and flash bulbs
during prayers, cannot be tolerated. .

On the other hand, if a video is being made of the ceremony, since those
cameras are silent in operation, the minister may permit of this to
continue (from a discreet distance) throughout the proceedings.

Marriage Certificates

A wide variety of these can be obtained from most good 'Gospel Bookshops' -
varying from the small and plain in a pad, to large and most decorative.

There's one in particular that I find exceedingly popular and appreciated
by couples - produced by C.R. Gibson, Publishers, of Norwalk, CT. 08856.
Ref. No. 387, available in packets of 24 each.

The same people also publish "The Marriage Service" in a small booklet form
which it is handy to use, and present to the bride after the service.   It
includes an attractive little Marriage Certificate, and additional pages in
which she can note 'Our Wedding Attendants', 'The Reception', and 'Guests',
etc.   It can be ordered by **Ref. H121**, available in boxes of 24 each.

Unfortunately, it is only produced setting down the 'Traditional' Marriage Service *in its modern version* and, moreover, also using the Lord's Prayer altered to read "And forgive us our debts, As we forgive our debtors" instead of in the original and, as far as I'm concerned, correct version.

Nevertheless, if one has a computer with a dot-matrix printer, one can very easily produce the original version of the vows, etc., [and of the Lord's Prayer] and paste these corrections over the existing pages - also paste in additional pages for any other required inserts, such as the Lesson.

If of course one is going to perform a marriage using only the *modern version* and without addition of a lesson as well - then this booklet will be found to be absolutely ideal for that purpose.

Second Marriages

If it is to be a second marriage only for the 'groom, and not for the bride then there is no reason why her plans for a beautiful wedding should remain unaffected by this.   If, however, it is a second wedding for the bride, it should be a much more modest one than the first - and the bride should most definitely *not* wear 'virgin' white, nor should she wear a bridal veil !

Frankly, unless the bride's previous marriage ended by an annulment, or she was widowed quite some considerable time ago, the more quiet and informal the wedding, the better.   If following a divorce or the death of the first spouse, it should be especially quiet - inviting only their close relatives and, very close friends to the wedding.   Incidentally, it is in bad taste for a widow not to put away her late husband's engagement and wedding rings when she becomes engaged to marry for the second time.

In spite of this, you will all too often find couples where one or the other (or even both) have only recently been divorced, having a 'big wedding' - with 'all the trimmings' - having no care for traditional standards of what is, and what is not appropriate behaviour in society.

You may even have a quite mature bride (accompanied by her several children) planning to wear a full 'virgin white' bridal gown !   As to whether or not you may agree to perform a marriage for such a brash individual - assuming that you cannot convince her that it would be far more seemly for her to be dressed in more appropriate ['reserved'] attire - shall be entirely within your own conscience and discretion to determine !

> I have had this happen !   Fortunately I heard about the bride's plans for her wedding (via a concerned third party) just in time.   In her enthusiasm and ignorance, she had not realized that she would almost certainly have been held up to ridicule at her wedding, and probably thoroughly embarrassed her (now 'grown up') children at the same time.

> That is to say, quite apart from exhibiting such a lack of reverence for the service in which she was to stand "before God" !   This event sharply reminded me to *always* raise the question of dress beforehand - as early as the initial Interview.

Whilst on the subject of children and second marriages: It is acceptable for a widow's, or widower's children of the first marriage to attend the second marriage of their surviving parent. However, young children of a first marriage should *not* attend the second marriage (of either parent), if the first had ended in divorce.

When a couple have been divorced, and wish to be reunited to each other in marriage again, no formal announcements or invitations should be sent out. The wedding should be quite private - and the family and friends advised of it, preferably afterwards, simply by letter or 'phone.

The Wedding Ring(s)

Sadly, all too often now one cannot tell a Wedding Ring from an Engagement Ring on the fourth finger of a woman's left hand ! Many Jewellers, not satisfied with selling a jewelled engagement ring, and subsequently a nice plain gold band for the wedding ring - are now actively promoting all sorts of 'combination rings' and the like, all jewelled, so that the wedding ring can no longer be recognized as such.

They are intentionally ignoring the fact that, the Wedding Ring should be "*a plain band* (preferably) *of gold*" which, once put on a bride's finger, should *never be removed* from her finger. It may be decorated by engraving but, it should not be 'jewelled', since it would then need to be removed from time to time, if only to be cleaned. If, when you interview a couple for marriage, the Wedding Ring has not yet been purchased - remind them !

To my astonishment, I have even found that in some Hospitals in the United States, when a woman is about to undergo surgery - the staff will remove a woman's wedding ring beforehand ! In the United Kingdom, from whence I hail, in all the hospitals of my experience there - they wouldn't think of doing such a terrible thing to her. They'll simply cover her wedding ring with a 'Band-Aid' plaster as a safety measure.

Mail romantic invitations - from "Romance" !

Did you know that, there is a town in Arkansas actually called "Romance" ?

If the Bride and 'Groom would like to add an unusual finishing touch (and a subject for conversation also) to the mailing of their Wedding Invitations, all they need to do is the following:

Having addressed all the envelopes and affixed the necessary postage - ready for mailing - then put the lot in one package addressed to: **The Postmaster, U.S. Postal Service, Arkansas 72136.**

He will know exactly what to do with all those invitations, and those to whom they're addressed will (at first anyway) be asking themselves *"Who do we know in......good gracious, where's that ?"* My apologies to the good folks who actually live in Romance, Arkansas, and of course know where they're at !

MINISTER'S MARRIAGES INFORMATION AND RECORDS

If you have your own Church and Parish, there should be nothing under this heading that you need to be told, about either your obtaining the necessary data you'll require from the bride and/or 'groom beforehand, or about the keeping of a permanent record after you have performed the marriage.

If you're a non-denominational (or other) minister without your own assigned church or other like establishment; this chapter will hopefully assist you in dealing with requests for you to perform marriages, making preparations beforehand, and subsequently maintaining records afterwards.

Confidential Questionnaire

For most, you'll probably first receive a 'phone call from either the bride or the bridegroom - sometimes a parent or friend first - at which time you can in any case obtain most if not all of the initial essential data you require. If on the other hand, the 'booking' is first received from such as a Referral Service, Wedding Center, Hotel, Restaurant, or Yacht Charter representative, you'll probably be advised of no more than the venue, day and time for the wedding and, a name and 'phone number to call for further details.

In any event, assuming you are in contact with one of the parties [bride or 'groom] you should immediately obtain the following information:

Date, Time, and Venue for the Wedding. If to be 'at sea' - estimated time of return from the cruise; The telephone number (as well as full address) for the venue.

Full name of Bridegroom, Denomination, Date of Birth, State or Country of Birth, Profession or Occupation, Home Address, Telephone Number [at Home and at Work]

Full name of Bride, Name at Birth (if different from present), Denomination, Date of Birth, State or Country of Birth, Profession or Occupation, Home Address, Telephone Number [at Home and at Work]

Full Name of Bride's Father [or whomsoever] 'giving' or presenting her for marriage.

Approximately how many Guests do they expect to attend the Wedding ?

If not already known - By whom was he/she referred to you for their Wedding ?

Do they require a Religious Service, or only a Civil Ceremony ? You can usually avoid going into further details over the 'phone as to precisely what sort of Religious Service, leaving that subject for discussion until you have **both parties** in front of you at interview.

Having done this, proceed to arrange a mutually convenient day and time for the couple to visit with you - as soon as possible - for an interview "to discuss the Order of Service, etc., required."

In the event that you are unable to obtain all of the above information more-or-less immediately over the 'phone, and/or if the couple cannot visit with you within the next two or three weeks at most - maybe they're calling from far away at this time, or not even coming into your area until shortly prior to the day of the wedding - you should promptly send them a "Confidential Questionnaire" - for completion and return to you as quickly as possible.

This should go a long way towards minimizing the need for any lengthy discussion later, which, if they cannot arrange to visit with you, may have to take place by telephone anyway.

There follows in **APPENDIX TWO** my suggested 'Form' for this purpose.

Table of Charges

For myself, I have a printed "Table of Charges" [for Baptisms, Weddings, Funerals, and Burials at Sea] on the reverse side of which there is added a brief mention of my own background and denomination, a few notes regarding different types of marriage services and, in particular, the following:

IMPORTANT - INTERVIEWS

THE CHAPLAIN WILL NOT CONSIDER ANY 'BOOKING' FOR HIS SERVICES AS BEING CONFIRMED, UNTIL SUCH TIME AS THE COUPLE TO BE MARRIED HAVE FIRST *MET WITH HIM IN PERSON* - USUALLY BY VISITING WITH HIM IN HIS HOME - AND THE 'ORDER OF SERVICE' ETC,, REQUIRED HAS BEEN *DISCUSSED AND AGREED UPON,* SUCH INTERVIEW TO IN ANY CASE BE ARRANGED AS SOON AS POSSIBLE *(PREFERABLY WITHIN TWO WEEKS)* AFTER FIRST 'BOOKING' [RESERVING] A DAY AND TIME WITH HIM FOR THE WEDDING,

UNDER NO CIRCUMSTANCES WHATSOEVER IS THE CHAPLAIN PREPARED TO PERFORM A WEDDING USING AN 'ORDER OF SERVICE' [e,g, A COUPLE'S "OWN SCRIPT"] THAT HE HAS NOT *FIRST APPROVED AND ACCEPTED* AT AN INTERVIEW WITH HIM - OR EXCEPTIONALLY, BY MAIL - NOT LESS THAN TWO WEEKS *PRIOR TO* THE DAY OF THE WEDDING,

PAYMENT OF THE CHAPLAIN'S (BASIC) FEE SHOULD BE MADE IMMEDIATELY UPON SATISFACTORY COMPLETION OF THE INTERVIEW - TO ALSO CONFIRM THE BOOKING, IN THE EVENT OF LATER CANCELLATION, SUCH FEE PAID SHALL NOT BE RETURNABLE IF CANCELLATION BE *RECEIVED LESS THAN ONE MONTH PRIOR TO* THE DATE BOOKED FOR THE WEDDING, HOWEVER, IN EXCEPTIONAL CIRCUMSTANCES [e,g, ILLNESS] THE CHAPLAIN MAY AGREE TO REFUND ALL OR PART OF THE FEE PAID, DEPENDING UPON SUCH CIRCUMSTANCES AND SEASON, ETC, IT SHOULD BE REMEMBERED THAT IT IS CUSTOMARY NOT ONLY FOR THE BASIC *FEE* TO BE PAID *IN ADVANCE* - BUT AN *"HONORARIUM"* TO BE HANDED TO HIM *AFTER* HE HAS PERFORMED THE SERVICE, THE CHAPLAIN'S *(BASIC) FEE* IS *INTENTIONALLY SET MUCH LOWER THAN MOST,* IN ORDER TO HELP COUPLES WHO HAVE ONLY A 'SMALL BUDGET' FOR THEIR WEDDING,

----
THESE NOTES ARE PRESENTED, RESPECTFULLY, FOR THE BENEFIT OF THOSE WHO MAY BE IN SOME DOUBT AS TO THE CORRECT PROCEDURE, AND TO AVOID EMBARRASSMENT BOTH TO THE MINISTER ATTENDING, AS WELL AS TO THEMSELVES, UNFORTUNATELY, WHEN DEALING WITH ALL THE ARRANGEMENTS AND EXPENSES FOR A WEDDING [e,g, VENUE, CATERING, DRESS HIRE, FLORIST, PHOTOGRAPHER, VIDEO, ETC,,] - THE MINISTER IS ALL TOO OFTEN THE LAST TO BE *CONSIDERED AND PROPERLY* TAKEN INTO ACCOUNT !

Much as it goes against the grain so to do, I strongly recommend that when you are dealing with couples who are not of your own congregation, and with whom you therefore do not already have an established relationship - you should ask for payment of your fee (to also 'firm up' the booking) upon satisfactory completion of the interview. If however, their booking is for many months ahead [some of mine are booked as much as an whole year or more in advance] then you need only require a suitable deposit, with the balance payable nearer the time of the wedding.

They have to pay a substantial deposit or even make full payment in advance to almost everyone else contracted for their wedding. And in the event of their later deciding to change their plans [e.g. to another date and time and/or venue, which you cannot make], or cancel altogether - they will certainly advise everyone else to whom they have made any payment, seeking a refund, but can be thoughtless enough not to contact you. That is to say, not unless they had made a payment to you in advance as well !

Meanwhile, you can have been refusing other couples being "already booked" and, not know anything of the cancellation - until you give them a courtesy call a few days before (what was to have been) their 'Wedding Day' to check and remind them not to forget to bring their Marriage Licence with them.

Record of Marriage

If you have a computer (or word processor) enabling you to keep all of your records, correspondence, etc., on Discs - so much the better. In any event, you will find it to your advantage to get all of the aforementioned data, and subsequently obtained information and/or arrangements agreed upon at the Interview, recorded on some sort of standard 'Form' that you can up-date as matters proceed to and beyond the Interview stage.

Also following in APPENDIX THREE, is my suggested 'Form' for this purpose.

These forms should be retained on file for at least five or six years - irrespective of whether or not there exists any requirement in your State for you to keep any records. If only for your own 'back reference' in the event of subsequent referrals arising later from family or friends in each case. If you don't have them on Computer Discs - and don't want to keep the actual paperwork itself on file, at least copy the essential data [Who, when and where, etc.] into a Journal or other suitable Notebook.

Included on these forms (or in your computer) you should also record both monies received and expenses incurred - to which you can refer when making your Income Tax Returns at the end of each year !

You will find it useful to indicate against each entry of a payment received - whether it was paid in cash or by cheque [check]. This will enable you to more easily check credits into your account at bank and, in the unhappy event of your suffering an I.R.S. Audit sometime, the Inspector will soon realize that you maintain an honest account of *all income* arising from your weddings etc., as well as of all your expenses. An Honorarium or gratuity received in cash after you have performed a wedding is taxable income, just as much as is your fee paid to you earlier by cheque !

FULL CEREMONIAL 'TRADITIONAL' CHURCH SERVICE

The 'Order of Ceremonial' and 'Order of Service' following in this chapter is taken largely (but not entirely) from the Marriage of His Royal Highness The Prince Charles and Lady Diana Spencer [H. R. H. The Prince and Princess of Wales] in St. Paul's Cathedral, City of London, on 29th July, 1981.

This includes, for *purposes of example only*, as the sort of 'Address' which one might use in such a full Service - being an edited version of that given by His Grace The Archbishop of Canterbury, Primate of All England, Dr. Robert Runcie, during the aforementioned Marriage Service.

Should you have occasion to perform a marriage; for which you have been requested to prepare a *truly comprehensive service*, perhaps in company also with other ministers, to be held in a church, and wherein the 'Register' [and Marriage Licence] is also to be signed during the course of the proceedings - rather than at some time and at some other place later - the following 'Order of Service' should provide you with adequate material *from which to draw inspiration !*

As previously stated, *this is not a verbatim transcript* of "The Royal Wedding" as such - much has been left out - being already *greatly modified* to nevertheless provide for a truly magnificent [but not 'regal'] event.

Perhaps for a Wedding where the bride and bridegroom are from different Parishes [but both nevertheless of like denominations] and in any case with their having a full retinue of 'attendants' [Bridesmaids, Pageboys, Grooms-men, etc.] included in the ceremonial ?

The 'Order of Ceremonial' in this case is of course British - with the bride and her father leading the processional instead of following - being the reverse order of that which is customary in many, if not most Weddings in the United States of America.

Order of Ceremonial

(A) Invited Guests and Family Members:

All invited guests should arrive and be seated well before the appointed time for the Wedding - dignitaries being escorted by Ushers to their assigned seating, in a reserved area immediately behind the front section reserved for family members.

Senior members of family [Parents, Grandparents, Brothers and Sisters not participating in the Processionals] shall then enter and be escorted by Ushers to their assigned places - Bride's family on the left-hand side of the aisle (facing the Altar) and Bridegroom's family on the right-hand side.   Their closest kin [e. g. Bride's Mother and Bridegroom's Mother and Father] to enter and be seated last.

Note: Front row seats are assigned with the seats closest to the aisle on each side for the fathers, and next to them, the mothers. [If divorced, fathers and mothers shall still be so seated and, their current spouses (if any) are to be seated discreetly elsewhere - if attending.]

(B)   Ecclesiastical Procession:

Essentially, this comprises the Choristers entering to take their places in The Chancel or Sanctuary Choir Stalls.

(C)   Processional - Bridegroom:

The Bridegroom, accompanied by his Main Supporter ["Best Man"] shall be the first (of the actual participants) to arrive at the church and proceed 'in procession' toward the Sanctuary - and thence to a place off to the right - to await the moment of taking their places at the steps before the Altar (immediately prior to the bride's processional) for the Marriage Service.

The 'Best Man' shall walk alongside and to the right of the 'groom. They may be led by 'Gentlemen Ushers' and followed by the second supporter and by senior (male) members of the bridegroom's household - such as his personal valet and private secretary.

Note;   The Bridegroom should not 'look around' to watch his bride approaching in processional (but may of course greet her quietly when she draws up alongside of him) and, they should not 'hold hands' at all !   That is to say, not until the moment when the Priest takes the bride's hand from her father and passes it to the 'groom to take - and make his vows to her,

(D)   Processional - Bride:

The Bride and her father [she being on his right arm] shall arrive next at the church and be greeted (upon entering the portico) by a Fanfare of Trumpets;   then to proceed 'in procession' up the aisle - followed first by her (preferably two or four) bridesmaids, next by (two) pageboys, then by her maid [or matron] of honour, and finally, by the bridegroom's other supporters [groomsmen].   **Not** also by any 'ushers' unless they are serving also as bridegroom's supporters.

Note;   Correctly, none of the bridesmaids, however young, should be referred to as 'Flower Girls',   Furthermore, in such a ceremonial, one does not have a 'Ring Bearer' - if the special honour of being included in the ceremonial is to be bestowed upon a young boy, he should be included therein as a Pageboy,   The Wedding Ring is to be carried by the bridegroom's main supporter ["Best Man"] - in an inside pocket,

For the 'Processional Music', in preference to the popular "Wedding March" in any of its various arrangements, one is much better recommended to have Jerimia Clarke's "Prince of Denmark's March" - "Trumpet Voluntary",

The Bride may **only** be preceded in her procession by an Ecclesiastical Group - if by anyone at all.

Note;   Following the arrival of the bride and her father at the Altar steps, the bridegroom's second supporter will supply the bridegroom and his main supporter with a copy of the 'Order of Service', as shall also the maid [or matron] of honour, supply the bride and her father with their copies of the Service - at the same time relieving the bride of her bouquet of flowers,

The entire party shall remain facing the Altar; the bridegroom's (two) supporters alongside (in line) and to his immediate right; the bride and her father (in line) to his immediate left; the bridesmaids and pages remaining in position behind the bride.

The maid [matron] of honour does not stand in line, but returns to her position in rear of the pages [to 'keep an eye on them ?]

(E) The Clergy:

The member(s) of clergy to officiate in the Marriage Service, having been standing in wait to one side, shall now come forward to face the couple and perform the marriage.   If there be two priests [ministers] performing the marriage;   first one shall say the 'introduction' [i. e. from "Dearly beloved..." to "...or else, hereafter forever hold his peace."] then the other priest [minister] shall charge the couple and proceed with the marriage itself.

Note: *If the couple are from different parishes, the Service should be held in the church for the bride's parish, with the priest [minister] in her parish having invited the bridegroom's priest [minister] to join with him in performing the marriage.*

(F) Signing the Register [Marriage Licence & Certificates]:

Upon the conclusion of the Marriage Service, the (two) priests shall lead the man and his wife to a Side Chapel [or Vestry] for the signing by witnesses of the necessary documents.   The bride shall be immediately followed by her maid [matron] of honour, who shall ensure that the train of her dress remains unentangled and flows smoothly.

At a respectable distance behind, then shall follow the bridegroom's parents, grandparents, his main and second supporters, and any other close kin [e. g. brothers and sisters].   Next the bride's parents and grandparents, etc.

After the signing, all except the bride and bridegroom shall return to their seats and, the bride's bouquet of flowers is returned to her in readiness for the Recessional.

(G) The Recessional:

The Bride and Bridegroom shall now reappear from the Side Chapel [or Vestry] to a Fanfare of Trumpets, still followed by the maid [matron] of honour - until reaching the main Aisle - at which point the bride and bridegroom shall be immediately followed in procession by first, the bridesmaids, then the pageboys, the bridegroom's main and second supporters, and the maid [matron] of honour.

At a short distance behind, shall then follow the bridegroom's mother escorted by the bride's father, next the bride's mother escorted by the bridegroom's father - and other close kin of both families.

Note: *Not until the entire 'Recessional' has cleared from the church may any other members of the congregation leave their seats to retire from the church. For the 'Recessional Music'; immediately following the Trumpet Fanfare, one is especially recommended to play Sir Edward Elgar's "Pomp and Circumstance" No. 4 in G.*

As an important footnote to all of the above, it should also be understood that whilst I have referred throughout to the "Maid [or Matron] of Honour", she should more correctly be referred to as the "Senior Attendant" - just as one does not have a "Best Man", but more correctly the "Bridegroom's Supporter", or if there be more than one; his "Main Supporter."

All of the terms "Best Man", "Maid (or Matron) of Honour", "Flower Girl", "Ring Bearer" and the like, although accepted in many churches [and almost universally elsewhere] in this present-day and age - especially in the United States - are nevertheless relatively 'modern' innovations, and **not** correct for use in any formal wedding ceremony in the Anglican Church.

The Order of Service

There follows in this chapter, a 'Traditional' Marriage Service adapted in all necessary respects - *whilst nevertheless retaining some of the changes made in the precise wording for the "Royal Wedding"* - to suit anyone who is desirous of having a similarly 'magnificent' and 'full ceremonial' Wedding.

Assuming that at least two members of the clergy are officiating, the First Minister shall make the 'Introduction' and, the Second Minister shall then proceed to perform the Marriage.

However, if the bride's father also happens to be a member of the clergy - albeit *not* of her parish and/or *not* from the church in which the marriage is to take place - then, he would escort his daughter in the Processional, and the 'host' minister would serve as the 'First' minister - but in this case right up to the point immediately following "Who giveth this woman to be married to this man ?" Her father having replied "I do" [or alternatively, such as "Her mother and I do."] he would then move into position in front of the couple, to proceed thenceforth as the 'Second' minister - and perform the actual marriage.

The Lesson may be read by the 'First' minister, or any appropriate invited dignitary or other guest - usually reading from the Lectern.

The Address should be given by the 'Second' minister - being the one who actually performed the marriage - usually reading from the Pulpit. However, it **may** alternatively be given by yet a 'Third' minister well known to one or other of the couple, invited by family to so honour the couple.

Supplementary Note (1992):

The fact that, sadly, H.R.H. The Prince and Princess of Wales have now finally decided to separate - although not divorce - does not in any way detract from the solemnity (and more importantly, the intent) of the Order of Service for the Solemnization of Holy Matrimony, from which much of the one following in this chapter was taken.

Unfortunately, even in the best of regulated unions between men and women, especially where both parties suffer the incredible stress and pressures that can be put upon their marriage, and indeed every moment of their private lives by others - some fail.

This case, as also in the case of H.R.H. The Duke and Duchess of York [Prince Andrew and the former Miss Sarah Fergusson] may serve (i) as a 'caution' and (ii) to evidence how much more difficult it can be for any couple to 'cope' with the strains that can arise in a marriage - where each party has been brought up within a very different sphere of social, financial, or religious surroundings and customs. Even moreso if one of them is used to being constantly "in the public eye" - and the other is not !

THE MARRIAGE SERVICE
[SOLEMNIZATION OF HOLY MATRIMONY]
THE ORDER FOR MARRIAGE
[TRADITIONAL]

129

[AS USED IN THE CHURCH OF ENGLAND]

Processional: *Prince of Denmark's March "Trumpet Voluntary" [Clarke]*

¶ *The couple shall stand **facing the Altar**, the man (and his supporters) to the right, the woman (and her father) to the left, other attendants behind.*

Hymn: *"Christ is made the sure foundation."*

THE INTRODUCTION

¶ *The [First] Minister shall say:*

> In the Name of the Father, and of the Son, and of the Holy Ghost. Amen.

¶ *Then addressing the congregation, he shall say:*

Dearly beloved, we are gathered here in the sight of God, and in the face of this congregation, to join together this man and this woman in Holy Matrimony, which is an honourable estate, instituted of God himself, signifying unto us the mystical union that is betwixt Christ and his Church, which holy estate Christ adorned and beautified with his presence and first miracle that he wrought in Cana of Galilee, and is commended in Holy Writ to be honourable among all men: and therefore is not by any to be enterprised nor taken in hand unadvisedly, lightly or wantonly; but reverently, discreetly, soberly, and in the fear of God, duly considering the causes for which matrimony was ordained.

First, it was ordained for the increase of mankind, according to the will of God, and that children might be brought up in the fear and nurture of the Lord, and to the praise of His holy Name.

Secondly, it was ordained in order that the natural instincts and affections implanted by God should be hallowed and directed aright; that those who are called of God to this holy estate, should continue therein in pureness of living.

Thirdly, it was ordained for the mutual society, health and comfort, that the one ought to have of the other, both in prosperity and in adversity; into which holy estate these two persons present come now to be joined. Therefore, if any man can show any just cause, why they may not lawfully be joined together, let him now speak, or else hereafter forever hold his peace.

THE MARRIAGE

¶ *The [Second] Minister addressing the persons to be married, shall say:*

I require and charge you both, as ye will answer at the dreadful day of judgement when the secrets of all hearts shall be disclosed, that if either of you know any impediment, why ye may not be lawfully joined together in Matrimony, ye do now confess it.   For be ye well assured, that so many as are coupled together otherwise than God's Word doth allow, are not joined together by God;   neither is their matrimony lawful.

¶   *If no sufficient impediment be alleged, the Minister shall say unto the man:*

_____, Wilt thou have this woman to thy wedded wife, to live together after God's ordinance in the holy estate of Matrimony ?   Wilt thou love her, comfort her, honour, and keep her, in sickness and in health;   and, forsaking all other, keep thee only unto her, so long as ye both shall live ?

¶   *Then the man shall answer:*

I will.

¶   *Then the Minister shall say unto the woman:*

_____, Wilt thou have this man to thy wedded husband, to live together according to God's law, in the holy estate of Matrimony ?   Wilt thou obey him and serve him, love him, comfort him, honour, and keep him, in sickness and in health;   and, forsaking all other, keep thee only unto him, so long as ye both shall live ?

¶   *The woman shall answer:*

I will.

¶   *Then the Minister shall say:*

Who giveth this woman to be married to this man ?

¶   *Then the Bride's father presenting her shall answer:*

I do.   [Alt: "Her mother and I do."]

The Vows

¶   *Then the Minister, receiving the woman at her father's hand, shall cause the man with his right hand to take the woman by her right hand, and to say after him as follows:*

I, _____, take thee, _____, to my wedded Wife, to have and to hold from this day forward, for better for worse, for richer for poorer, in sickness and in health, to love and to cherish, 'till death us do part, according to God's holy law;   and thereto I plight thee my troth.

¶   *Then shall they loose their hands;   and the Minister shall cause the woman with her right hand to take the man by his right hand, and to say after him as follows:*

I, _____, take thee, _____, to my wedded Husband, to have and to hold from this day forward, for better for worse, for richer for poorer, in sickness and in health, to love, cherish and to obey, 'till death us do part, according to God's holy law; and thereto I give thee my troth.

The Ring Ceremony

[A]----------------------If Only One Ring Be Used-------------------------

¶   *The Minister shall now secure the Wedding Ring from the Bridegroom's Supporter ['Best Man'] who shall place it upon the book held by the Minister, who shall say:*

Bless, O Lord, this Ring, and grant that he who gives it, and she who shall wear it, may remain faithful to each other, and abide in thy peace and favour, and live together in love until their lives end, through Jesus Christ, our Lord.   Amen.

¶   *The Minister will now hand the Ring to the man, who places it on the woman's fourth finger of her left hand and,* **holding it there,** *shall say after the Minister:*

With this ring I thee wed;   with my body I thee worship;   and with all my worldly goods I thee endow: In the name of the Father, and of the Son, and of the Holy Ghost.   Amen.

[B]------------------------If Two Rings Be Used--------------------------

¶   *The Minister shall now secure the Wedding Ring from the Bridegroom's Supporter ['Best Man'] and the Second Ring from the Senior Bridesmaid [Maid (or Matron) of Honour], who shall each in turn place the Rings upon the book held by the Minister, who shall say:*

Bless, O Lord, these Rings, and grant that they who shall wear them, may remain faithful to each other, and abide in thy peace and favour, and live together in love until their lives end, through Jesus Christ, our Lord.   Amen.

¶   *The Minister will now hand the Wedding Ring to the man, who places it on the woman's fourth finger of her left hand and,* **holding it there,** *shall say after the Minister:*

With this ring I thee wed;   with my body I thee worship;   and with all my worldly goods I thee endow: In the name of the Father, and of the Son, and of the Holy Ghost.   Amen.

¶   *The Minister will now hand the Second Ring to the woman, who places it on the man's fourth finger of his left hand and,* **holding it there,** *shall say after the Minister:*

With this ring I thee wed: In the name of the Father, and of the Son, and of the Holy Ghost.   Amen.

¶   *Then the Minister shall say:*

Let us Pray.

O Eternal God, Creator and Preserver of all mankind, Giver of all spiritual grace, the Author of everlasting life;   Send thy blessing upon these thy servants, this man and this woman, whom we bless in thy Name, that living faithfully together, they may surely perform and keep the vow and covenant betwixt them made, whereof this ring [*these rings*] given and received is a token [*are tokens*] and pledge, and may ever remain in perfect love and peace together, and live according to thy laws;   through Jesus Christ our Lord.   Amen.

¶ *Then shall the Minister join their right hands together and say,*

Those whom God hath joined together let no man put asunder,

¶ *Then shall the Minister speak unto the company,*

Forasmuch as _____ and _____ have consented together in holy wedlock, and have witnessed the same before God and this company, and thereto have given and pledged their troth, either to other, and have declared the same by giving and receiving of a Ring, and by joining of hands;   I pronounce that they be Man and Wife together, in the Name of the Father, and of the Son, and of the Holy Ghost. Amen.

¶ *Then the Man and the Wife kneeling, the Minister shall add this Blessing,*

God the Father, God the Son, God the Holy Ghost, bless, preserve, and keep you;   the Lord mercifully with his favour look upon you, and so fill you with all spiritual benediction and grace, that ye may so live together in this life, that in the world to come ye may have life everlasting. AMEN.

Anthem: *"Let the people praise thee, O God;   Yea, let all the people praise thee."*   [Psalm 67.]

The Lesson

¶ *Then shall the [First] Minister [or whomsoever else may be chosen for this] shall read the Lesson, which he shall take from First Corinthians, Chapter 13, Verses 1 to 13, - from The New English Bible - as follows:*

"I may speak in tongues of man or of angels, but if I am without love, I am sounding gong or clanging cymbal.   I may have the gift of prophecy, and know every hidden truth: I may have faith strong enough to move mountains; but if I have no love, I am nothing.   I may dole out all I possess, or even give my body to be burnt, but if I have no love, I am none the better.

Love is patient;   love is kind and envies no one.   Love is never boastful, nor conceited, nor rude;   never selfish, not quick to take offence.   Love keeps no score of wrongs;   does not gloat over other men's sins, but delights in the truth.   There is nothing love cannot face; there is no limit to its faith, its hope, and its endurance.

Love will never come to an end.   Are there prophets ? their work will be over.   Are there tongues of ecstasy ?   they will cease.   Is there knowledge ? it will vanish away;   for our knowledge and our prophecy alike are partial, and the partial vanishes when wholeness comes.   When I was a child, my speech, my outlook, and my thoughts were all childish.   When I grew up, I had finished with childish things.   Now we see only puzzling reflections in a mirror, but then we shall see face to face.   My knowledge now is partial;   then it will be whole, like God's knowledge of me.

In a word, there are three things that last for ever: faith, hope, and love; but the greatest of them all is love."

Thanks be to God.

The Address

N.B.   This is taken almost verbatim (with only necessary deletions) from Dr. Robert Runcie's address at the Wedding of H.R.H. The Prince and Princess of Wales - not of course to be used by any minister (unless at least giving due credit to its author beforehand) but, more as an indication of the subject matter, and guide from which to gain inspiration for a minister's own personal address to suit the couple concerned.

¶   Then the [Second] Minister, addressing the congregation, **may** say:

Here is the stuff of which Fairy Tales are made;   a couple on their Wedding Day;   but Fairy Tales usually end at this point with the simple phrase "they lived happily ever after."   This may be because Fairy Tales regard marriage as an anti-climax after the romance of courtship.   This is not the Christian view;   our faith sees the wedding day not as the place of arrival but the place where the adventure really begins.

There is an ancient Christian tradition, that every bride and 'groom, on their wedding day are regarded as a Royal couple.   To this day, in the marriage ceremonies of the Eastern Orthodox Church;   Crowns are held over the man and woman to express the conviction, that as husband and wife, they are Kings and Queens of creation.   As it says of human kind in The Bible: "Thou crownest him with glory and honour and didst set him over the work of thy hands."

On a Wedding Day, it is made clear that God does not intend us to be puppets, but chooses to work though us, and especially through our marriages, to create the future of His world.   Marriage, is first of all a new creation of the partners themselves;   as husband and wife live out their vows, loving and cherishing one another, sharing life's splendours and miseries, achievements and set-backs, they will be transformed in the process.

A good marriage is a life, as the poet Edmund Muir says: "Where each asks from each, what each most wants to give, and each awaits in each what else would never be."   But any marriage which is turned in upon itself, in which the bride and 'groom simply gaze obsessively at one other, goes sour after a time.   A marriage which really works, is one which works for others;   the marriage has both a private face and a public importance.   If we solved all our economic problems and fail to build loving families, it would profit us nothing.   Because the family is the place where the future is created good, and full of love, or deformed.

Those who are married, live happily ever after the Wedding Day, if they persevere in the real adventure, which is the 'Royal' task of creating each other, and creating a more loving world.   That is true of every man and woman undertaking marriage.

Much of the world is in the grip of hopelessness;   many people seem to have surrendered to fatalism, about the so-called inevitabilities of life, cruelty, injustice, poverty, bigotry, and war.

Some have accepted a cynical view of marriage itself; but all couples on their Wedding Day are 'Royal' couples, and stand for the truth that we help to shape this world, and are not just its victims. All of us are given the power to make the future more in God's image, and to be Kings and Queens of love. This is our prayer for _____ and _____.

May the burdens we lay on them, be matched by the love with which we support them in the years to come, and however long they live, may they always know, that when they pledged themselves to each other before the Altar of God, they were surrounded and supported, not by mere spectators, but by the sincere affection and the active prayer of many, many friends.

Thanks be to God.

¶ Then the [First] Minister, **and the people,** standing, shall **say the Lord's Prayer.**

Our Father, which art in heaven, Hallowed be thy Name. Thy kingdom come. Thy will be done, On earth as it is in heaven. Give us this day our daily bread. And forgive us our trespasses, As we forgive them that trespass against us. And lead us not into temptation, But deliver us from evil. For thine is the kingdom, and the power, and the glory, for ever and ever. Amen.

¶ Then the [First] Minister may add this Blessing:

Almighty God, the Father of our Lord Jesus Christ, call upon you the riches of His grace, sanctify and bless you, that you may please Him both in body and soul, and live together in holy love, until your lives end. Amen.

Hymn: "I vow to thee my country..." [Gustav Holtz]

¶ Then the [Second] Minister may add this Blessing:

God the Holy Trinity, make you strong in faith and love, defend you on every side, and guide you in truth and peace, and the blessing of God Almighty, the Father, the Son, and the Holy Spirit, be amongst you and remain with you always.

Choir shall sing the: **"Amen."**

Anthem: "Let their celestial concerts all unite." [Handel] –

¶ – During which the Husband and Wife, and their Witnesses, shall proceed to the place designated for the signing of the Church Register [Marriage Licence and Certificates] – following which, the witnesses shall return to the body of the Church and await the re-entry of the bride and 'groom [to a Fanfare of Trumpets], to there join and follow them in the Recessional.

Recessional: "Pomp and Circumstance" No. 4 in G. [Elgar]

—— T. 6.

Note: Whilst it may be customary elsewhere, it is NOT correct for the minister to 'present' the couple upon completion of the service to the congregation ["Mr. & Mrs. ...."] and neither should the minister invite the bridegroom to "kiss the bride" !!!

EQUALITY - OR DISUNITY ?

It is all too evident in the present-day attitudes and relationships between men and women, that the word "equality" has been taken to have different meanings to different people.   One consequence of this has been that these different understandings of "equality" have been a source of division and disunity - not only within the public sector, but also within our homes.

I am reminded of Catherine, wife of the late **Reverend Doctor Peter Marshall,** a boy from quite humble beginnings in Scotland who emigrated to America and eventually became the Chaplain of the Senate, and pastor of the "Church of Presidents" in Washington, D.C.

The then Miss Catherine Wood, as a young girl from West Virginia, was at a somewhat raucous "Young People's Meeting" in Atlanta, where Peter wanted to hear what young people thought, and called for volunteers to speak. Inspired by the sermons she had heard of his in church, she accepted the challenge, mounted the platform and, straight 'off the cuff', said this:

> *"I would like to talk, as a girl, to the girls here this afternoon; I know that if you boys will listen, they'll listen too.   And I'm just as sure that the only reason they've been just as rude and silly as you've been, is because they have the mistaken idea that you wanted them to be.*
>
> *I never thought much about being a girl until about two years ago, when I learned from a man, what a wonderful thing it is to be a woman. Until that Sunday morning, I considered myself lucky to be living in the Twentieth Century; the century of progress and emancipation. The century when, supposedly, we women came into our own; but I had forgotten, that the emancipation of woman really began with Christianity - when a girl, a very young girl, received the greatest honour in history.*
>
> *She was chosen to be the mother of the saviour of the world.   And when her son grew up and began to teach his way of life, he ushered woman into a new place in human relations.   He accorded her a dignity she had never known before, and crowned her with such glory, that down through the ages, she was revered, protected, and loved.   Men wanted to think of her as different from themselves;   better, made of finer, more delicate clay.*
>
> *It remained for the Twentieth Century, the century of progress, to pull her down from her throne.   She wanted equality.   For nineteen hundred years she had not been equal;   she had been superior.   To stand equal with men, naturally she had to step down.   Now, being equal with men, she has won all their rights and privileges - the right to get drunk, the right to swear, the right to smoke, the right to work like a man, to think like a man, to act like a man.   We won all this, but how can we feel so triumphant, when men no longer feel as romantic about us as they did about our grandmothers ?   When we've lost something sweet and mysterious, something that is as hard to describe as the haunting whistful fragrance of violets.*

Of course, these aren't my original thoughts;   they are the thoughts I heard that Sunday morning, but from them, some thoughts of my own were born.   And the conclusion reached, that somewhere along the line, we women got off the track.   Poets have become immortal by remembering on paper, a girl's smile;   but I've never read a poem rapsodizing over a girls' giggles at a smutty joke, or ever heard a man brag about his sweetheart or his wife that she could drink just as much as he and become just as intoxicated.   I have never heard a man say that a girl's mouth was prettier with a cigarette hanging out of it, or that her hair smelled divinely of stale tobacco.   That's all I have to say;   I've never made a speech before."

The audience quietened down almost immediately she started speaking, sat listening intently to every word;   and rose to loudly cheer her afterwards.

Catherine made these remarks many years ago in this 'enlightened' twentieth century, the 'century of progress.'   Since then, on balance, have women gained any greater respect from men, or do men look upon them now as 'equals' - whom they can 'kick around' much as they might any other men ? Look at the divorce rates;   the ever-increasing numbers of single-parent families;   at sexual harassment in the workplace.   And consider the cases of rape reported almost daily in the news !

You may care to make a copy of her speech and, if you think it appropriate, show it to any prospective bride and her fiancee.   You may be pleasantly surprised by their reaction.

There are many women who would dearly love to be properly respected as ladies, not just as women, and have all men treat them as ladies again.

SETTING EXAMPLES FOR OUR CHILDREN

Consider also, the examples we're setting for our children.   They can hear all around them at almost every level in society, business, and politics, of so many 'special interest' groups loudly insisting upon **only their own** views being recognized and held supreme - selfishly determined to achieve their own ends, often by fair means or foul - whether they're causing harm, loss or hardship to anyone else or not !

When I hear some youngsters, determined to do whatever **they** want to do, and claiming as their "right" to do whatever they please, I'm frequently having to point out to them that: their "rights" must end, where someone else's "rights" begin, and vice-versa - otherwise there's 'war' !

There is all too often a parallel to this in the home, if children observe any bickering between their parents, where one of them is being inconsiderate of the other - by some selfish act or decision.

Peter Marshall, making his first invocation in the U.S. Senate, said:

"Our Father in heaven, we pray for the members of this body, in their several responsibilities;   make them see dear Lord, that you're not the God of any one party, of any one nation, or of any one race. Teach us that freedom may be seen, not as the right to do as we please,

but as the opportunity to do what is right.   Give us the courage to stand for something, lest we fall for anything.

Save us from hot-heads that would lead us to act foolishly, and from cold feet, that would keep us from acting at all.   Create new warmth and love between the members of the senate, so that they may go at their work not head first, but heart first.

Help us our Father, to show other nations an America to imitate;   an America that loves fair play, honest dealing, straight talk, real freedom and faith in God.   Help us make this God's own country by living like God's own people.   Amen. "

This Prayer is as appropriate today as it was then, in fact even moreso, not only for those whom we send to represent us in Washington, D.C., but for **every one of us** in our daily lives.   Not least of all, whenever we have to make any decision or take any action, that could affect anyone else in addition to ourselves.

Christ taught us to "Love thy neighbour ..."   It's not always easy to love **all** of our neighbours, **all** of the time - but we can try.   How can we do this ?   Work and live, *to the very best of our ability*, according to His teaching, and God's commandments !

THE TEN COMMANDMENTS

I have met people who, having broken one or more of the Ten Commandments, have somehow imagined that they were therefore now 'damned' - especially if they have done so several times - and thus being 'beyond redemption' they might just as well carry on as before.

Not so !   I tell folks it's my belief that, when God handed down to Moses those commandments, he did so as 'ten good rules' to live by as well as we can, as constantly as we can.   He didn't really expect all of us, to keep all of them, all of the time.   He knew that as ordinary weak human beings, almost all of us would fail to some extent from time to time.

Find me a Priest who can honestly swear that even he has **never** broken at least one of the Ten Commandments [in thought or deed] sometime during his lifetime.   If you can, he (or she, since we now also have women with us in the clergy) must be a Saint !

I then add that, if you are truly sorry about what you have done [or "ought to have done, and have not done"] and you are going to do your very best henceforth, difficult as it may often be, not to repeat the offence - then God **will** forgive you.

On the other hand, if you choose to continue to sin as before, as if with impunity, then you had better be prepared to live the rest of your life not only "in the **love** of God" - but also "in the **fear** of God" !

Personally, as an Anglican, I do not believe that it will suffice simply to go into the Confessional [e.g. as in the Roman Catholic Church], confess to a Priest, and do whatever penance he then requires of you - in order to be

'let off the hook'.   Neither does it help simply to contribute more money,
[and perhaps even some of your ill-gotten gains ?] to your Church.   Your
Church may benefit, but you won't.   You cannot *buy* your way into God's
grace.   Especially if, when tempted and deciding that you *want* to commit a
sin, you look upon this, as sadly too many do, as an easy way for you to
'wipe clean the slate' afterwards.

You might feel 'good' about it for awhile but, think about it.   Isn't that
far too easy to make any sense ?

-oOo-

"Marriage Laws"

Summary of State Marriage Laws - paraphrased to advise who can perform marriages, and what is required of you to perform marriages and/or subsequent to performing a marriage in the State.

ALABAMA   Any licenced minister of the gospel in regular communion with the Christian church or society of which he is a member, may perform marriages.   Also, marriages may be performed by the pastor of any religious society according to the rules of the religious society.

Ministers must provide a Certificate of Marriage to the Judge of Probate within one month after the marriage.

For questions see the clerk for the Judge of Probate.

ALASKA   The minister, priest or rabbi of any church or congregation in the state may perform marriages.

Ministers must provide Marriage Certificates to the couple married and report the marriage to the Marriage Commissioner.

*   For questions see the Marriage Commissioner.

ARIZONA   Any licenced or ordained clergyman may perform marriages.

Ministers must record the marriage on the Marriage Licence and return it to the clerk of the Superior Court within 20 days after the marriage.

For questions see the clerk of the Superior Court.

ARKANSAS   Any regularly ordained minister or priest of any religious sect or denomination may perform marriages.

Ministers must have their ordination credentials filed by the County Clerk who will then issue a certificate to the minister.

The Marriage Licence must be completed by the minister and returned to the County Clerk within 60 days from the date the licence was issued.

*   For questions see the County Clerk.

CALIFORNIA   Any priest, minister, or rabbi of any religious denomination, of the age of 18 years or over, may perform marriages.

Ministers must complete the Marriage Licence and return it to the County Clerk within 4 days after the marriage.

For questions see the County Clerk.

COLORADO   Marriages may be performed by any minister.

Ministers must send a Marriage Certificate to the County Clerk.

For questions see the County Clerk.

CONNECTICUT   All ordained or licenced clergymen belonging to this State or any other
                 State may perform marriages as long as they continue in the work of the
                 ministry,

                 Marriage Licence must be completed by the minister and returned to the City
                 or Town Clerk,

                 For questions see the City or Town Clerk,

DELAWARE   Any ordained minister of the gospel and every minister in charge of a
                 recognized church may perform marriages,

                 Ministers do not need to be licenced to perform marriages but they must
                 report their name and address to the local registrar in the district in
                 which they live,

                 Ministers must keep the Marriage Licence or a copy for at least one year,
                 Also the minister must, within 4 days, complete and return the forms
                 required by the State Board of Health to the Clerk of the Peace,

        *   For questions see the Clerk of the Peace,

FLORIDA   All regularly ordained ministers of the gospel in communion with some
                 church may perform marriages,

                 Ministers must complete a Certificate of Marriage on the Marriage Licence
                 and return it to the office from which it was issued,

                 For questions see the County Clerk,

GEORGIA   Any minister who is authorized by his or her church may perform marriages,

                 Ministers must complete a Certificate of Marriage and return it to the
                 ordinary within 30 days after the marriage,

                 For questions see the ordinary's clerk at the County Courthouse,

HAWAII   Any minister may perform marriages if they are authorized by their church
                 to do so,

                 Ministers must obtain a licence from the Department of Health before
                 performing marriages,

                 Ministers must keep a record of all marriages they perform,   Ministers
                 must report all marriages they perform, to the Department of Health,

        *   For questions see the Department of Health,

IDAHO   Marriages may be performed by priests or ministers of the gospel of any
                 denomination,

                 Ministers must give a Marriage Certificate to the bride and to the 'groom,
                 Also, the minister must complete the Licence and Marriage Certificate and
                 return it to the recorder who issued it, within 30 days after the marriage,

For questions see the County Recorder.

ILLINOIS   Marriages may be performed by ministers of the gospel in regular standing in the church or society to which they belong.

The Marriage Licence and Certificate must be completed by the minister and returned to the County Clerk within 30 days after the marriage.

For questions see the County Clerk.

INDIANA   Ministers of the gospel and priests of every church throughout the State may perform marriages.

Ministers must return the Marriage Licence and Certificate of Marriage to the Clerk of the Circuit Court within 3 months after the marriage.

*   For questions see the Clerk of the Circuit Court.

IOWA   Ministers of the gospel who are ordained by their church may perform marriages.

Ministers must give a Certificate of Marriage to the bride and to the 'groom. Also, the minister must report the marriage to the Clerk of the District Court within 15 days after the marriage.

For questions see the Clerk of the District Court.

KANSAS   Any ordained clergyman of any religious denomination or society may perform marriages.

Ministers are required to file credentials of ordination with the judge of a Probate Court before performing marriages.

Ministers must return the Marriage Licence and a Certificate of Marriage to the Probate Judge who issued the Marriage Licence, within 10 days after the marriage.

*   For questions see the Clerk of the Probate Court.

KENTUCKY   Marriages may be performed by any minister of the gospel or priests of any denomination with any religious society.

Ministers must be licenced before performing marriages. See the local County Clerk for a licence.

Ministers must return the Marriage Licence and Marriage Certificate to the County Clerk within 3 months after the marriage.

It is illegal to solicit marriages.

*   For questions see the County Clerk.

LOUISIANA   Ministers of the gospel or priests of any denomination in regular communion with any religious society may perform marriages.

Ministers must register with the Clerk of the District Court of the parish, or with the Health Department if in New Orleans.

(Louisiana)   After performing a marriage, the minister must complete a Marriage Certificate and return it to the Clerk of the District Court.

*   For questions see the Clerk of the District Court.

MAINE   Ordained ministers of the gospel may perform marriages.

Ministers must be licenced by the Secretary of State before performing marriages.   Application may be made to the Town Clerk or Treasurer. There is a (small) fee to be paid.

After the marriage, the minister must file a copy of the Record of Marriage with the Town Clerk.

*   For questions see the Town Clerk.

MARYLAND   Ministers of the gospel authorized by the rules and customs of their church may perform marriages.

Ministers must complete the Marriage Licence and Marriage Certificate and give one certificate to the couple.   Another certificate and the licence must be returned to the Clerk of the Court of Common Pleas, within 5 days after the marriage.

For questions see the Clerk of the Court of Common Pleas.

MASSACHUSETTS   Ordained ministers of the gospel may perform marriages.

Before performing marriages, ministers are required to apply for a certificate from the State.   For applications write to: The Commonwealth of Massachusetts, Office of the Secretary, Supervisor, Commissions Division, State House, Boston, Massachusetts 02133.   You must file a copy of your Ordination Certificate and a statement from (your) church saying that you are in good standing.

Ministers must keep records of all marriages they perform.   Also, ministers must return a Certificate of Marriage to the Town Clerk or Registrar who issued the Marriage Licence and to the Town Clerk of the town where the marriage was performed.

*   For questions see the Town Clerk or Registrar or write to the Secretary of State.

MICHIGAN   A minister of the gospel who is ordained or authorized by his or her church to perform marriages and who is a pastor of a church in this State, or continues to preach the gospel in this state, may perform marriages.

Ministers must complete a Marriage Certificate and give one to the couple. Another Marriage Certificate must be returned to the County Clerk who issued the licence, within 10 days after the marriage.

*   For questions see the County Clerk.

MINNESOTA   Any licenced or ordained minister of the gospel in regular communion with a religious society may perform marriages.

Ministers must file a copy of their credentials of ordination with the Clerk of the District Court of any county.

Ministers must give a Marriage Certificate to the bride and 'groom and also file a certificate with the Clerk of the District Court in the county which issued the Marriage Licence.

*   For questions see the Clerk of the District Court.

MISSISSIPPI   Any ordained minister of the gospel who is in good standing with his or her church may perform marriages.

Ministers must send a Certificate of Marriage to the clerk who issued the Marriage Licence, within three months after the marriage.

For questions see the Clerk of the District Court.

MISSOURI   Marriages may be performed by any clergyman *who is a citizen of the United States* and who is in good standing with any church or synagogue in this State.

Ministers must keep a record of all marriages they perform. They must give the couple a Marriage Certificate and must complete the Marriage Licence and return it to the Recorder of Deeds, within 90 days after the Marriage Licence was issued.

*   For questions see the Recorder of Deeds.

MONTANA   Ministers of the gospel of any denomination may perform marriages.

Ministers must complete and return a Marriage Certificate to the clerk of the District Court within 30 days after the marriage. Also, the minister must provide Marriage Certificates to the bride and 'groom upon request.

For questions see the Clerk of the District Court.

NEBRASKA   Any ordained clergyman whatsoever, without regard to the sect to which they may belong may perform marriages.

Ministers must report marriages they perform to the Court Judge who issued the Marriage Licence, within 15 days after the marriage. Also the minister must provide Marriage Certificates to the bride and 'groom upon request.

For questions see the County Clerk.

NEVADA   Any ordained minister in good standing with his denomination, whose denomination is incorporated or organized or established in the State of Nevada may perform marriages.

Ministers are required to complete a complicated procedure to obtain a "Certificate of Permission" to perform marriages.   Among other requirements, the applicant's ministry must be primarily one of service to his congregation or denomination and his performance of marriages must be incidental to such service.

*   For questions (and applications) see the County Clerk.

NEW HAMPSHIRE   Marriages may be performed by any ordained minister of the gospel who resides in the State and is in good standing with his church.   Ministers not residing in the State may obtain permission to perform a marriage upon application to the Secretary of State.

Ministers must send a copy of the Marriage Certificate to the Town Clerk.

*   For questions see the Town Clerk.

NEW JERSEY   Every minister of every religion may perform marriages.

Ministers must complete a Certificate of Marriage and return it to the County Clerk.

For questions see the County Clerk.

NEW MEXICO   Any ordained clergyman whatsoever, without regard to the sect to which he or she may belong may perform marriages.

Ministers must provide the County Clerk with a Marriage Certificate within 90 days after the marriage.

For questions see the County Clerk.

NEW YORK   Marriages may be performed by a clergyman or minister of any religion.

CAUTION;   However, a 1972 Court Case said that in order for a marriage to be valid, the minister must have an actual church or at least a stated meeting place for worship or any form of religious observance.

Ministers do not have to be licenced except that, before performing marriages in New York City, the minister must register his or her name and address in the office of the City Clerk of the City of New York.

Ministers must complete a Marriage Certificate and return it to the Town or City Clerk who issued the Marriage Licence, within 5 days after the marriage.

*   For questions see the Town or City Clerk.

NORTH CAROLINA   Any ordained minister of any faith who is authorized to perform marriages by his church may do so.

Ministers must complete the Marriage Licence and return it to the Registrar of Deeds who issued it.

For questions see the Registrar of Deeds.

NORTH DAKOTA   Ordained ministers of the gospel and priests of every church may perform marriages.

Ministers must file a Certificate of Marriage with the County Judge who issued the licence, within 5 days after the marriage. Certificates must also be given to the persons married.

For questions see the County Clerk.

OHIO   Any ordained or licenced minister of any religious society or congregation within this State may perform marriages.

Before performing a marriage, ministers must present their ordination credentials to the Probate Judge of any County. The judge will provide the minister with a licence to perform marriages. The minister must then present his licence to the Probate Judge in any County in which he performs a marriage.

Ministers must send a Certificate of Marriage to the Probate Judge of the County which issued the Marriage Licence within 30 days after the marriage.

*   For questions see the Clerk of the Probate Court.

OKLAHOMA   Ordained ministers of the gospel of any denomination, who are at least 18 years of age, may perform marriages.

Ministers must file a copy of their credentials with the County Clerk before performing marriages.

Ministers must complete a Certificate of Marriage and return it to the clerk or judge who issued the licence.

*   For questions see the Clerk of the County Court.

OREGON   Ministers of any church organized, carrying on its work, and having congregations in this State may perform marriages in this State if authorized by their church to do so.

Before performing marriages, ministers must file their credentials with the County Clerk of the county in which they reside or in which the marriage is to be performed.

Ministers must give the bride and 'groom a Marriage Certificate upon request. Also, the minister must send a Marriage Certificate to the County Clerk who issued the Marriage Licence, within one month after the marriage.

*   For questions see the County Clerk.

PENNSYLVANIA   Ministers of any regularly established church or congregation may perform marriages. Also, persons may marry themselves if they obtain a certificate from the Clerk of the Orphan's Court.

Ministers must provide a Certificate of Marriage to the bride and 'groom. Also, they must send a Marriage Certificate to the Clerk of the Orphan's Court who issued the Marriage Licence, within 10 days after the marriage.

For questions see the Clerk of the Orphan's Court.

RHODE ISLAND

Everyone who has been, or is, the minister of any society professing to meet for religious purposes, or incorporated for the promotion of such purposes, and holding stated and regular services, and who has been ordained according to the customs and usages of such society may perform marriages.

Ministers must obtain a licence from the City or Town Clerk before performing marriages.

Ministers must endorse and return the Marriage Licence to the City or Town Clerk in which the marriage was performed.

✻ For questions see the City or Town Clerk.

SOUTH CAROLINA

Ministers of the gospel who are authorized to administer oaths in this State may perform marriages.

Ministers must complete the Marriage Licence and give one copy to the parties and the other two must be returned to the County Judge of Probate who issued it, within 15 days after the marriage.

✻ For questions see the County Judge of Probate or his clerk.

SOUTH DAKOTA

Marriages may be performed by a minister of the gospel, or priest of any denomination.

Ministers must provide the bride and 'groom with Marriage Certificates upon request. Ministers must also keep a Record Book of all marriages they perform. Finally, the minister must send a Marriage Certificate to the clerk who issued the Marriage Licence, within 30 days after the marriage.

For questions see the Clerk of Courts.

TENNESSEE

All regular ministers of the gospel of every denomination, and Jewish Rabbis, more than 18 years of age, having a care of souls may perform marriages.

Ministers must endorse the Marriage Licence and return it to the Clerk of the County Court within 3 days after the marriage.

For questions see the County Clerk.

TEXAS

Ordained Christian ministers and priests, Jewish rabbis and persons who are officers of religious organizations and who are duly authorized by the organization to conduct marriage ceremonies, may perform marriages.

Ministers must complete the Marriage Licence and return it to the County Clerk who issued it, within 30 days after the marriage.

For questions see the County Clerk,

UTAH   Ministers of the gospel or priests of any denomination who are in regular communion with any religious society may perform marriages.

Ministers must provide a Certificate of Marriage to the County Clerk who issued the Marriage Licence, within 30 days after the marriage.

For questions see the County Clerk,

VERMONT   Ordained ministers residing in this State may perform marriages.   Non-resident ordained ministers may perform marriages with the permission of the Probate Court of the District within which the marriage is to take place.

Ministers must complete the Marriage Licence and Certificate of Marriage and return it to the clerk's office from which it was issued, within 10 days from the date of the marriage.

*   For questions see the Town Clerk,

VIRGINIA   Ministers of any religious denomination may perform marriages.

Before performing marriages, ministers must provide proof of their ordination and proof that they are in regular communion with their church to the Circuit Court of any county or city or to the Corporation Court of any city in this State.   The judge will then authorize the minister to perform marriages provided the minister obtains a Bond in the amount of five hundred dollars [$ 500.00.]

Ministers may receive a fee of no more than ten dollars [$ 10.00.] for performing a marriage.

Ministers must complete the Marriage Certificate and return it to the clerk who issued the Marriage Licence, within 5 days after the marriage.

*   For questions see the Clerk of the County Circuit Court or the Clerk of the Corporation Court,

VIRGIN ISLANDS Clergymen or ministers of any religion, whether they reside in the Virgin Islands, or elsewhere in the United States, may perform marriages.

Ministers must complete the Marriage Licence and return it to the Clerk of the Municipal Court which issued the licence, within 10 days after the marriage is performed.

For questions see the Clerk of the Municipal Court,

WASHINGTON   Regularly licenced or ordained ministers or any priest of any church or religious denomination anywhere within the State may perform marriages.

Ministers must send two Certificates of Marriage to the County Auditor within 30 days after the marriage.

For questions see the County Auditor.

WASHINGTON D.C.   Ordained ministers of the gospel may perform marriages.

Marriage Licences are addressed to the minister who will perform the ceremony.   The minister must complete a Marriage Certificate for the bride and for the 'groom and return another certificate to the Clerk of the District of Columbia Court of General Sessions within 10 days after the marriage.

For questions see the Clerk of the Court of General Sessions.

WEST VIRGINIA   Any minister, priest, or rabbi, over the age of 18 years, may perform marriages.

Before performing marriages, ministers must provide proof of their ordination to the clerk of any County Court.   The clerk will then provide the minister with an order authorizing him or her to perform marriages.

Ministers must return the completed Marriage Licence to the County Clerk who issued it on or before the 5th day of the month following the marriage.

*   For questions see the Clerk of the County Court.

WISCONSIN   Any ordained clergyman of any religious denomination or society may perform marriages.

Before performing marriages, ministers must file their credentials of ordination with the Clerk of the Circuit Court in the county in which their church is located.   The clerk will give the minister a certificate.

Ministers must complete the Marriage Certificates and give one to the bride and one to the 'groom.   The original must be returned to the Register of Deeds of the county in which the marriage was performed or if performed in a city, to the City Health Officer.   This must be done within 3 days after the marriage.

*   For questions see the Clerk of the Circuit Court.

WYOMING   Every licenced or ordained minister of the gospel may perform marriages.

Ministers must give a Marriage Certificate to the bride and 'groom upon request and must return a certificate to the County Clerk.

For questions see the County Clerk.

*   There exist various limitations and/or arrangements to be made in these States in particular before you can commence performing marriages therein.   In most if not all others, seemingly any Minister can go there from out-of-State and perform a marriage service, without any restrictions or preliminary formalities whatsoever.

IMPORTANT

1.   In the State of KENTUCKY, it is illegal to solicit marriages.

2.   In the State of MISSOURI, you must in any case be a citizen of the United States; it will not suffice to be a legal resident [e.g. Resident Alien holding a 'Green Card']

3.   In the State of VIRGINIA, you are required to obtain a Bond in the amount of $ 500.00, and yet you may receive a fee of no more than $ 10.00, for performing a marriage !

ACKNOWLEDGEMENT

The entire content of 'Appendix One' is from material compiled (after many hours of research in the Law Library acquiring this information) by the AMERICAN FELLOWSHIP CHURCH, and for the kind provision of which the Author is especially grateful.

It is believed to be accurate and reliable (although not necessarily infallible) and, whilst it is reproduced in good faith now in this publication for your guidance, you must *act upon it entirely at your own risk,* and should in any case check with the appropriate authorities for any changes.

NOTES — CHANGES

APPENDIX TWO

MINISTER'S CONFIDENTIAL QUESTIONNAIRE

[See Chapter Fifteen]

WEDDING PLANS – MINISTER'S QUESTIONNAIRE

[CONFIDENTIAL]

THE MINISTER REQUESTS THAT THIS QUESTIONNAIRE BE COMPLETED BY THE COUPLE PLANNING TO BE MARRIED – AND RETURNED TO HIM *BY FIRST CLASS MAIL* AS SOON AS POSSIBLE. AN APPOINTMENT SHOULD BE MADE TO MEET WITH THE MINISTER IN PERSON, TO DISCUSS SUCH MATTERS AS "THE ORDER OF SERVICE" ETC, REQUIRED – PREFERABLY WITHIN TWO WEEKS AFTER BOOKING [RESERVING] A DAY AND TIME WITH HIM FOR THE WEDDING – IN ORDER TO CONFIRM THE BOOKING. N.B. UNDER NO CIRCUMSTANCES WHATSOEVER IS THE MINISTER PREPARED TO PERFORM ANY WEDDING USING A "SERVICE" THAT HE HAS NOT *FIRST APPROVED AND ACCEPTED* AT AN INTERVIEW WITH HIM, OR, EXCEPTIONALLY, BY MAIL – NOT LESS THAN TWO WEEKS *PRIOR* TO THE DAY OF THE WEDDING.

VENUE FOR THE WEDDING

PLACE: _____

PHONE: (   )_____ DATE: _____ TIME: _____

THE BRIDE

_____
NAME – FIRST (Given)   MIDDLE   CURRENT LAST (FAMILY) NAME

_____
DATE OF BIRTH – Month, Day, Year   LAST NAME (AT BIRTH) IF DIFFERENT

_____
STATE (OR COUNTRY) OF BIRTH   RELIGIOUS DENOMINATION

_____
RESIDENCE – Street and Number   CITY   STATE & ZIP

(   )_____   (   )_____
TELEPHONE (Residence)   TELEPHONE (Work)

STATE PROFESSION/OCCUPATION: _____

BRIDE TO BE GIVEN/PRESENTED BY: _____
                          FULL NAME OF FATHER (or Friend)   RELATIONSHIP

THE 'GROOM

_____
NAME – FIRST (Given)   MIDDLE   LAST (FAMILY) NAME

_____
DATE OF BIRTH – Month, Day, Year   PROFESSION/OCCUPATION

_____
STATE (OR COUNTRY) OF BIRTH   RELIGIOUS DENOMINATION

_____
RESIDENCE – Street and Number   CITY   STATE & ZIP

(   )_____   (   )_____
TELEPHONE (Residence)   TELEPHONE (Work)

THE GUESTS

NAME OF MATRON/MAID OF HONOUR: _____
                                          FULL NAME   RELATIONSHIP

NAME OF GROOM'S SUPPORTER ["BEST MAN"] _____
                                          FULL NAME   RELATIONSHIP

RING BEARER (IF ANY)_____
                                   FULL NAME   RELATIONSHIP

FLOWER GIRL (IF ANY)_____
                                   FULL NAME   RELATIONSHIP

NOTE: IF YOUR WITNESSES ARE TO BE *OTHER THAN* (1) THE MATRON/MAID OF HONOUR, AND
        (2) THE 'BEST MAN', PLEASE STATE NAMES OF THE WITNESSES BELOW:

_____
        NAME OF WITNESS No. 1.   RELATIONSHIP

_____
        NAME OF WITNESS No. 2.   RELATIONSHIP

APPROXIMATE NUMBER OF GUESTS ATTENDING THE WEDDING/RECEPTION ? _____ / _____

THE MARRIAGE SERVICE

TYPE OF SERVICE PREFERRED: _____
                         *   TRADITIONAL OR MODERN [CATHOLIC OR PROTESTANT]
                               NON-DENOMINATIONAL, INTER-FAITH, SECULAR [CIVIL]

ONE OR TWO RINGS ? _____   DRESS - FORMAL OR INFORMAL ? _____

MINISTER TO WEAR - CHAPLAIN'S UNIFORM, CLERICAL or CIVILIAN DRESS ? _____

ORDER OF SERVICE TO INCLUDE: * THE LESSON ? _____   * CANDLE CEREMONY ? _____
                                              YES/NO   YES/NO

        * THE WINE-CUP CEREMONY ? _____   * THE BENEDICTION ? _____
                                 YES/NO   YES/NO

OTHER SPECIAL REQUIREMENTS/REQUESTS ? _____

_____

HAVE YOU ALREADY OBTAINED A 'LICENSE' ? _____   DATE OF ISSUE: _____
                                        YES/NO   MONTH-DAY-YEAR

WHERE ISSUED ? _____   TYPE ? _____
                     COUNTY   REGULAR OR CONFIDENTIAL

CEREMONY: _____   CONGREGATION/COMPANY: _____
              HELD INSIDE OR OUTSIDE   TO SIT OR STAND

MUSIC ? _____   MINISTER TO 'PRESENT' COUPLE ? _____
          LIVE, D.J., RECORDED, OTHER   YES/NO
----

* THESE QUESTIONS CAN BE DISCUSSED IN MORE DETAIL WITH THE MINISTER AT INTERVIEW

APPENDIX THREE

WEDDING BOOKINGS AND RECORD

[See Chapter Fifteen]

WEDDING BOOKING & RECORD
[SOLEMNIZATION OF HOLY MATRIMONY]

```
              AT:  ...................
                   .........................
              TEL:  (    ) ...  ....
        .....DAY, ................, 199..
           ..... - ..... HOURS
```

```
Bridegroom:        Mr.                          Denom:
                                                DoB:
                                                State:
                                                Tel:


Bride:             Miss                         Denom:
                                                DoB:
                                                State:
                                                Tel:


Bride given by:    M                            Tel:
```

```
'Groom's Occupation:
Business / Industry:                            Tel:

Bride's  Occupation:
Business / Industry:                            Tel:
```

```
Couple's Address:
[After Marriage]

                                                Tel:
```

===

```
Order of Service:

Reading/Lesson:
Blessing:
Rings:             One or Two ?                 Dress:    Formal ?
Other Notes:

Reception at:                                   Tel:

                                                No of Guests:

Photographer:                                   Tel:
Videographer:                                   Tel:
```

```
Referred by:                                    Date:
                                                Ref:

Officiating:       Rev.
Dress [Minister]:
```

===

```
Licence No:        ......... [Regular or Confidential ?]
Issued Date:       ......... [City of.................]
Filed [by Mail]:   ......... [................. County]
```

```
Certificates:      Service Booklet, Regular Cert, Special (Large) Cert, State Cert.
```

===

==
Interviews, etc:

> [A standard form of this nature can be set up in a computer, with different
> 'stock' headings for each of the venues at which you may be regularly performing
> marriages, thus enabling you to quickly up-date (and print-out afresh) after each
> contact and/or as and when additional data/instructions may be received.]

==
Minister's Remarks:
  [Closing File]

> [Here you may wish to note enquiries received for your services in the future
> from family and other guests at the Wedding (e.g. for Weddings, Baptisms, etc.)
> Also to 'rate' the occasion as an whole and, the families in particular - for
> future reference in event of any referrals subsequently arising therefrom]

==
Fees/Donations:	$		[**Basic (Minimum) Fee**] Payable *in advance* at Interview
	+ $		[**Honorarium to Minister**] Customary *after* the Ceremony
Travel - Car:	$		[@ 25¢/mi. - if in XS of 20 mi. from Minister's Office]
Certificates, etc.	$	n/c	[Gratis per Minister]
TOTAL RECEIVED:	$		

Less Expenses:	$		[Car - ___ miles @ 25¢/mi.]
	$		[Service Booklet, Certificates, Filing of Licence, etc.]
NET INCOME:	$		**Folio Ref:**
==

THE DEVELOPMENT OF THE CHRISTIAN CHURCHES

For the uninformed, the following will provide a simplified 'family tree'
showing the development of the Christian Churches - to the present day.

```
                              THE EARLY CHURCH
                                    *
                          Early schisms and heresies
                                    *
        THE CHURCH OF              The Great Schism (1054)           THE ORTHODOX
      + + ROME (WESTERN) < * * * *  dividing the Church into Western  * * * * > (EASTERN) CHURCHES
      +       *                    and Eastern Churches              RUSSIAN
      +       *                                                      GREEK
      +     * * * * > * * * *                                        SYRIAN
      +             *                                                ARMENIAN
      +     The Reformation (16th c,)                      COPTIC (Egyptian & Ethiopian)
      +             *                                                +
      +     * * * * * * < > * * * * * * * * * * *                  + + + + + + +
      +       *         *                   *                                  +
      + Martin Luther   John Calvin     Thomas Cranmer   John Wesley      William    +
      + (1483-1546)     (1509-64)       (1489-1556)      (1703-91)        Booth      +
      +       +             +                +               +               +        +
      +    LUTHERAN      CALVINIST      * * < * * ANGLICAN * * > WESLEYANISM * * * > SALVATION +
      +    CHURCHES      REFORMED       *      CHURCHES     (Methodism)      ARMY (1878) +
      +       +          CHURCH         *         +             +               +        +
      +       +             +           *         +             +               +        +
      +       +             +           *         + ) * * *     +  + + + + + + +         +
      +       +    * * * < +            *         +      *      +  +                     +
      +     + + +     *     +      CONGREGATIONAL +      *      +  +                     +
      +       +       *     +      CHURCHES       +      *      +  ============          +
      +       +     * * *   +         +           George Fox  +  +  NEW CHRISTIAN        +
      +       +     *       +         +              +         +  +  GROUPS IN THE        +
      +       +     *    PRESBYTERIAN +         RELIGIOUS      +  +    U.S.A.             +
      +       +     *    CHURCHES     +         SOCIETY OF     +  +  [See Note 1.]       +
      +       +     *       +         +         FRIENDS        +  +  ============        +
      +     BAPTIST +       + + + + + + + +     [Quakers]      +  +                      +
      +     CHURCH  +             + +                          +  +                      +
      +       +     + + + + + + + + + + + + + + + + + + + + +  +  CHURCH OF             +
      +       +               + + + +                         +  SOUTH INDIA            +
      +       + + + + + + + + + + + + + + + + + + + + + + + +     [See Note 2.]          +
      +       +               + + + + +                              +                  +
      +     + + + + + + + + + + + + + + + + + + + + + + + + + + + + + + + + + +         +
      +                 + + + + + + +                                                   +
      +                 + + + + + + + +                                                 +
  Roman Catholic        + + + + + + + +                                                 +
  Vatican               + + + + + + + +                                                 +
  Council <Exchange Observers>  WORLD COUNCIL OF CHURCHES + + + + + + + + + + + + + + + + + + + + +
```

(1)   Including: Church of Jesus Christ of Latter Day Saints [Mormon]; Seventh-Day Adven-
      tist Church; Church of Christ Scientist; Disciples of Christ; Churches of Christ,
(2)   Union of Methodist, Presbyterian, Congregational, Reformed and Anglican Churches,

* >   Movements of Division,
+ +   Movements of Reunion,

NOTES